INSIDE
THE KGB

BY

ALEKSEI MYAGKOV

ARLINGTON HOUSE·PUBLISHERS
NEW ROCHELLE, NEW YORK

363.2017
M995i

Second Printing, November 1977

Copyright © 1976 by Aleksei Myagkov

First American Edition

Manufactured in the United States of America

Library of Congress Cataloging in Publication Data

Myagkov, Aleksei, 1945-
   Inside the KGB.

   1. Russia (1923-   U.S.S.R.). Komitet
gosudarstvennoĭ bezopasnosti. I. Title.
HV8225.M9   363.2   77–8016
ISBN 0–87000–389–5

3|78

CONTENTS

CHAPTER 1

A watchdog slips the leash

IT was six o'clock in the morning. I, a Captain of the Special Department of the Soviet Committee of State Security, the KGB —a counter-intelligence officer—was in my office located at the headquarters of a Motorised Rifle Regiment which was part of the Soviet forces stationed in East Germany. My direct responsibility was to safeguard the security of this regiment against the *internal* enemies of the USSR and the Western intelligence services.

What had brought me at such an early hour to my office? I was getting ready to flee to the West. This would take place the same afternoon, and while I still had a little time, I was checking over and over again that nothing had been forgotten: a briefcase with secret documents; a pistol, in case my plan ran into difficulties; a waterproof cape, which I could wear under my officer's greatcoat, so that I could disguise myself as a civilian.

Together with a group of officers from the regiment for which I was responsible, I was about to leave in uniform by bus in 15 minutes for West Berlin, where I planned to make my escape. Ostensibly the officers were going to West Berlin for a stroll in the town, but in reality to study the military installations of the American, British and French garrisons.

As an officer of the Special Department of the KGB, my rôle was to safeguard their security; not to protect them from the plottings of Western "aggressors", but to prevent any one of them fleeing to the West. This was officially the reason for my presence in the bus, but here I was, a Soviet officer, leaving the country of "happiness, equality and brotherhood" for the world of "rotting Capitalism". The urge to leave one's homeland would be unnatural to people in most countries, but the governments of the Soviet bloc—with the exception of Yugoslavia—keep their citizens locked in. Communist régimes try in every conceivable way to prevent anyone escaping from Communism. For this reason alone, the loud pronouncements about "happiness, equality and brotherhood" at once become suspect.

My thoughts on the bus were disturbed by the jokes and the conversation of the officers who were with me. Some were just talking; others cracking jokes. A young lieutenant, a doctor, and incidentally a KGB agent recruited by me and used for keeping an eye on his own comrades, declared in a loud voice which could

1

be heard by all in the bus: "It would be nice if we were allowed in West Berlin to get out of the bus near a pornographic shop, so that we could get some interesting magazines." Approving murmurs were heard and all looked in a questioning way at me. I said jokingly to the lieutenant that I would have to forbid him trips to the West, as he was susceptible to Capitalist influences and indiscreet in his relations with women. One of the officers added: "Ah Misha, you have forgotten that a counter-intelligence chap is sitting here and you may find yourself in gaol."

Everyone laughed, including me, though there was little to laugh about. The lieutenant was trying to put things right and shouted to me: "Comrade Captain, on orders from the Party, I am ready to forget all women! " All laughed, and a major, who sat not far from me, joined in the conversation, saying: "You, Misha, are behaving as in the joke in which a citizen was asked under what circumstances he would sit on a hedgehog with a bare bottom. After thinking, he replied: 'If the hedgehog was shaved, if the bottom was someone else's, or if it was Party orders'." The major's last words were drowned in general laughter.

In the bus, besides this lieutenant there were two other KGB agents who kept a watch on me. One of them, a captain, was sitting next to me. He noticed my briefcase, pointed to it and asked in a voice that could be heard by all: "Comrade Captain, your briefcase probably contains secret documents which you are intending to hand over to the West?"

"The devil has got into your mind," I thought, "if only I could knock your block off." Aloud I said: "Of course, secret documents, what else could it be." All smiled contentedly; it did not enter any-one's head that that was really the case. Someone commented that my briefcase contained a tape-recorder and that I was recording all their chatter. There was no more talk on this subject.

I sat and thought: "If only you knew, captain, that your joke was true." My thoughts were diverted by our crossing the frontier of East Berlin to the West. It was the American Control Point. An American soldier stopped our bus, counted the number of people in it and we went on into West Berlin. There we passed military instal-lations of our "allies" and made two stops.

The first stop was at the Charlottenburg Palace, where the officers were permitted to get out of the bus and be photographed; entry to the building, while this was going on, was forbidden.

The second stop was at the Soviet monument, located not far from the Brandenburg Gates.

For my escape, there was only one possibility, the stop at the Charlottenburg Palace. My plan was to stray away from the group;

go into the park next to the Palace and hide my greatcoat and service cap there. In the waterproof cape, which was under my greatcoat, I would look like an ordinary civilian. After that, all I had to do was to take a taxi and get to the Americans. But things do not always work out as planned.

We arrived at the Palace, the officers left the bus and started to take photographs. I stood not far from them, holding my briefcase. The situation was such that I could not go into the park without being seen. Though the distance to it was only about 100 metres, the group of officers was standing about in such a way that the route to the park, which I had to cross, was constantly under their observation. For this reason, I gave up my original plan and at once started to look for another possibility.

I decided to enter the Palace and go out of its back door into the park. But how could I get into the building without being noticed? I looked around. The officers were still taking photographs and no one paid any attention to me. Seizing the opportunity, I slipped into the building. As far as I could make out, no one had noticed me; otherwise I would have had to bring out my pistol, and this I wanted to avoid. But as the saying goes, fortune favours the brave, and, in this case, I was lucky.

In the Palace, a museum had been arranged and there were some visitors. I paid no attention whatever to all this. It was essential to act quickly, as my absence would soon be noticed by the officers. And so, I walked faster and faster. I had to find the emergency exit from the building into the park. But I was not alone; there were streams of visitors in the museum. I had to go slowly to the first floor, and pass casually through the house, while inside I was like a coiled spring. There was not a second to lose, but I could not find the exit into the park. Then suddenly—a door! I looked around, made sure that no one was watching and then quickly passed through the door into a room. A key was protruding from the inner side of the door. I locked it and then looked around to get my bearings. Around me were pictures, picture frames and . . . yet another door! I was on the point of checking whether this second door would open, when I heard a rustling noise in one of the corners, which was hidden from me by a picture. I moved across and found a small table at which an old German was sitting, eating. Seeing me, he started in surprise and asked in a Berlin accent: "Man! Who are you? Have I gone dotty? Surely you are a Russian?"

"Everything is all right, daddy," I said, "enjoy your meal," and at the same time, despite the seriousness of the situation, I burst out laughing. I think no one could have helped laughing at seeing the bulging eyes and strained face of the German.

I asked him whether there was an exit into the park from the building. He replied in the affirmative and nodded in the direction of the second door. On the old man's table I saw a telephone. "Why not get in touch over the telephone with the police and with their help make my next move," I thought. "Of course, that's the only way." I asked the German to ring the police; tell them that a Soviet officer was seeking political asylum and ask them to send a car as soon as possible to the back entrance of the Charlottenburg Palace. The old man did so immediately, then wanted to leave the room. This was not to my liking, for the possibility could not be excluded that he might tell the Soviet officers about me. So I told him politely and firmly: "Give up all idea of leaving the room until the police arrive. Sit here and remain quiet." I added that the door of the room was locked, and that the key was in my possession. The old man submitted to my demand without protest; he even declared that he had no wish to leave me alone and would remain with pleasure. I was glad to have an ally and praised him for his courage.

I now had to prepare for the next stage. I took off my greatcoat and service cap and hid them behind a picture. I then put on my civilian cape which concealed my uniform. I went to the window, which had a curtain drawn over it, and looked carefully out into the street. I could see the bus and the officers, who were talking excitedly among themselves. Some of them pointed to the building in which I was hiding.

I looked at my watch; it was exactly twelve o'clock. It was clear that the senior Soviet officer had reported by radio what had happened to Berlin-Karlshorst, and after half an hour, KGB groups would start looking for me in West Berlin. If I failed to get to the police during that critical half hour, my situation would become dangerous. Something must be done, but what? I again turned my attention to the second door, and began to pull on the handle. It was locked. I looked in my pockets for something that might turn the lock and felt the key from the first door. Would it match the lock? Yes, it did. I opened the door, looked along a corridor, and told the old man that I would return soon. Having locked the door after me, I walked along the corridor. At the end of it, I saw some stairs and went down them to the ground floor. At the bottom was a heavy door, I opened it, and . . . found myself at the back of the building. Pleased with my discovery, I returned to the room.

Where are the police? Why are they dawdling so long? I told the old man to ring them once more and hurry them up. He did so and said the police would soon arrive.

I looked at the time again: it was 12.30. For me, that was now the only hope. I could not go outside again, as the KGB groups searching for me must be somewhere in the vicinity. In my heart I cursed the police for their slowness. The German looked at me with sympathetic eyes. I thanked him for his understanding.

It was already 13.00. I decided to go via the park into the town and then get myself a taxi to the Americans. At that moment, I heard someone's footsteps along the corridor. The thought passed through my head—what if it was the KGB? I got out my pistol; released the safety catch and opened the door sharply. In the corridor, I saw two men in civilian clothes, who, on seeing me, stopped dead in their tracks with startled looks. "Police," shouted one of them. He showed me his identification and asked me to put away my weapon. Relieved, I pocketed it; returned to the room; said goodbye to the German; picked up my greatcoat and service cap and left the building through the back entrance with the police. I got into their car and after only some three minutes, we were at a police station.

It turned out that the police station was opposite the Charlottenburg Palace. I complained that they had taken up so much valuable time on such "an important and complicated" operation as crossing the street. The policemen said that that did not depend on them, as they had to get in touch with the British, and report everything to them, and it was only after getting permission that they could collect me.

At the station, I felt more confident. While I was there, the KGB could not take any action against me. But it was premature to rejoice, for I still had to get from the police station to a British military unit, and that was not without risk.

The police turned out to be quite hospitable. They offered me coffee and said that I would have to wait again, this time for the arrival of the British Military Police. This wait lasted until 14.00 hours—a whole hour. All this made my situation considerably more dangerous, for with each minute more and more KGB men would appear in West Berlin. But there was nothing else I could do but wait. The Charlottenburg Palace and the bus with the Soviet officers could be seen from the window of the police station. The doors of the bus were closed and the officers sat in their places. A Volga car with a Soviet registration number stood near the bus. All this confirmed once more that an active search was going on.

The police tried to distract me from my anxious thoughts. They questioned me about Russia, what the weather there was like and so forth. They displayed great curiosity about my military uniform. Some of them asked for a souvenir. I had to cut off two buttons from my greatcoat and hand them over. Similar requests for souvenirs were granted more than once in the future.

At last a British Army sergeant and two privates turned up. He appeared to be about 40 to 45 years of age, short, and not at all like a military type, giving a homely impression. He had a kind face, which, for some reason, looked apologetic. Moreover, his right foot was in plaster. Limping, he approached me, and in broken Russian asked if I really wished to remain in the West. I replied in the affirmative, adding that one did not play about on such matters; it could cost me my life.

The sergeant asked me if I was armed. I unfastened my tunic and reached for my pistol, which was under my left arm. The sergeant, noticing the movement, jumped aside, waved his arms and said that I was not to touch my weapon. I understood that he feared what I might do and laughingly invited him to take the pistol himself. I remarked that perhaps he thought I belonged to some organisation such as the Arab terrorist organisation Black September and was about to start a war with the Western world. The sergeant made no reply, but one could see that he was embarrassed.

After that, the four of us, the sergeant, two privates and I, made for the exit. In the station yard I made a disagreeable discovery, my rescuers had arrived in a military police car coloured green, with military signs and numbers, and a warning light. Only a fire engine could have been more conspicuous. It would not be difficult for the searching KGB groups to identify such a car and determine where I was. But I had no choice; we got into the car and went off. After five minutes, we noticed that we were being followed. Without attempting to conceal their purpose, the KGB agents' cars accompanied us right up to the entrance of the British military unit.

I was escorted into the Military Police building and put into a small room simply furnished with a bed, table and three chairs. The window was covered by a metal grill.

One of the soldiers remained in the room with me all the time. I could not even visit the toilet without being accompanied. At 16.00 hours, an official appeared and informed me that London was aware of my case and that I would soon be sent further West. I inquired why the situation around me was so tense. He explained that my presence at the military unit was comparable with an atom bomb ready to go off any minute, and added: "The Russians are near, the KGB is everywhere. Any kind of provocation can be expected and, therefore, it will be best for everyone if we get you out of here as quickly as possible."

After his departure, a sympathetic captain appeared and said he would remain with me. A soldier brought me a towel and shaving kit.

The captain explained that about 22.00 to 23.00 hours, we would be flown to the West, and that until then we would have to remain where we were. He said that the KGB had observation points around the British unit and for this reason, we could only get to the aerodrome by helicopter, as a journey by car would be dangerous.

We chatted about all manner of insignificant things. Then I pointed to the packet of razor-blades for the safety razor, saying jokingly: "You are guarding me so well, and then you yourselves bring me razor blades. What if I cut my veins with one of these blades?" However, my joke was not to the captain's liking. He looked at me curiously, then called a private and ordered him to remove the blades. At about 22.30, two bundles of civilian clothing were brought in for the captain and myself, and we were asked to change. I was then briefed about the next moves. At 23.00, we were to leave the building and get into a car, in which I must sit between two escorts. The car would take us to the helicopter in which I, with one of my escorts, would be taken to the airfield where a plane would be waiting.

These precautionary measures were taken because of the very real risk of an attack by Soviet agents who might try and kidnap me. The British had alerted one of their units to strengthen security during the operation.

We left the building; got into the car; drove 50 metres and stopped at the helicopter, which was waiting with its engine running. Around us could be seen British soldiers in full battle-dress, with automatic weapons in their hands and tense faces. With the captain, we got into the helicopter quickly and it took off immediately.

After about ten minutes, we landed next to an aircraft and again we lost no time in getting into our seats. Within five minutes, we were flying to the West.

With me were two escorts and two pilots. Their expressions were tense and I did not feel very relaxed either. The aircraft we were in was of Second World War vintage and had a maximum speed of only 280 kms per hour. We were flying over the territory of East Germany and, despite our two escorting fighters, there was a real chance of being shot down by a Soviet missile "by accident". At last the long flight over East Germany was over, and as we crossed the frontier into West German airspace, the atmosphere in the aircraft brightened noticeably. Everyone began to smile and the captain congratulated me on my safe arrival in the West.

At about four o'clock in the morning, we reached our destination at last. It was not far from Dusseldorf. The British received me warmly; it was evident that they understood my agitation, and we were all happy that the greatest danger was over, though not all the problems had yet been solved.

On the day after my arrival in the West—I escaped on 2 February 1974—a diplomatic war began over my body. Soviet diplomats waged it with all the power at their disposal.

On the first day, Soviet representatives demanded categorically several times to be given facilities to meet me in person. And every time, they were informed by the British of my refusal to have such a meeting, not because I was afraid, but simply because I did not see any purpose in it. I had no intention of returning, nor any wish to encounter threats and lies. So the first day passed.

The second day dawned. Up to twelve o'clock no one disturbed me except two nice children, the son and daughter of the host and hostess of the apartment. The girl was about seven, and the boy one year younger. They were amused that an unknown uncle was speaking in a strange language and did not want to leave my side. This helped to distract me from unpleasant worries.

At twelve o'clock, the British passed me another offer from the Soviet side. If I would return, they said, I would be forgiven: a strange offer. In the first place, I had no intention of returning to the unjust system from which I had just escaped. Secondly, I knew only too well how the KGB and the whole Soviet system went about forgiveness: if strictly carried out it would mean prison, Siberia, and the usual outcome: execution. Of course, my answer was "No".

The third day brought yet another bit of news. This time three British representatives came to see me and I was told: "The Soviet side accuses you of being guilty of a criminal offence. We await your official reply."

My answer was that I had not committed any criminal offence. "Moreover," I added, "only yesterday the Soviet side itself did not accuse me of anything and made an offer for me to return, which surely confirms that I am not a criminal." The British were satisfied with my answer. With that, the diplomatic war by the Soviet Union ended. For me, a new life in the West had begun. But it is premature to write about it. In the first place, I want to relate what forces compelled me, a Russian counter-intelligence officer, to leave my native country and join the émigrés.

CHAPTER 2

Indoctrination and disillusionment

I WAS born in 1945, in a small village in central Russia. My parents were ordinary peasants. The family was a fairly large one, three girls and three boys, of whom I was the eldest. Soon after my birth, our family moved to a small town, Lebedyan, with a population of about 30,000, where I spent my childhood.

Lebedyan is an ancient Russian town, dating back to before the time when Russia was under the Tartar yoke. The centre of the town lies on a hill which at one time served as a defence against the Tartars. Later, when their grip was finally broken, the population increased and new streets branched out from the centre. The old names of the streets (Archers, Gunners, Cossacks) indicated the military nature of the town as one of the country's defensive garrisons. Now, they have been renamed Ulitsa (street of) Lenina, Karl-Marx Street, and so on. The town is rich in ancient customs, passed down from one generation to another.

Among the male population great importance is still attached to such qualities as courage, strength and daring. The town is divided symbolically into districts which compete with one another, each out to demonstrate that its menfolk predominate in all these desirable qualities. Rival claims are tested in sporting events, such as tug-of-war and weight lifting. The culminating events in these competitions are the "fisticuff" bouts. In accordance with old tradition, these take place once a year at "maslenitsa" (Shrovetide).

The male inhabitants of both districts, from the age of 18 upwards, assemble on a grass plot and form up into two rows opposite one another, ready for the fight. Unwritten rules lay down that during individual clashes, it is strictly forbidden to make use of such things as bits of wood, stones, or even ordinary gloves. In accordance with tradition, the fight is started by two teenage boys. This clash between them serves as a signal for the adults awaiting the brawl, for each side wants their particular boy to emerge as the victor.

When the single combats between the boys end, the rows of men close in and the fisticuffs begin. The one who falls to the ground is considered to have been defeated and departs, if capable of walking, from the field of battle. Some fall into the arms of women spectators who give them first-aid treatment. The winning district is the one that loses the least combatants and forces the "enemy" to surrender.

9

After the battle, the recent rivals, with black eyes, stroll off with arms around each other's shoulders.

Such traditions naturally made a great impression on us boys. The qualities that were most appreciated by us were dexterity, courage and strength. These were demonstrated in various ways, for instance by going fearlessly down the highest hill on skis, by swimming faster than anyone else across a river, or by emerging victorious from a tussle with another individual. I succeeded fairly often in emerging as the victor from the clashes and in other forms of self-defence, so that I enjoyed some prestige among the youthful inhabitants of the district, although it meant that I often had to return home with black eyes. This did not bring forth any expressions of sympathy. It merely prompted my father to ask: "Well, tell me my hero—did your enemy after the fight also become 'coloured' or not?" After getting a reply in the affirmative, he would say: "The most important thing after these clashes is that you should bear no malice towards each other and remain fair and upright."

To complain at home about anyone with whom one had had a tiff was considered by us boys to be the greatest of crimes, and anyone who broke this rule—even once—lost the respect of his comrades for ever. It was in this way that I, like most of my contemporaries, spent much time out of doors among a circle of friends.

There was another side of my childhood: the conflict between school and home education. The crux of this was that the Russian people have been educated down the ages in a religious spirit, and up to the time of the October Revolution, the Orthodox Church played a big part in their lives. After the Revolution, with the arrival of the Communists, a campaign was started against believers in the Church, who were subjected to persecution in various ways. However, despite all their efforts the Communists have failed to eradicate religion and Christianity in Russia.

Up to the time of the Revolution, there were many churches in our town; during my childhood only one church remained in being for the whole town and area, the others being turned into stores, shops and even clubs. Those who visited this one church were shadowed and dubbed by Party functionaries as backward and "deluded" people. But despite all this, there were many believers in our town. Therefore, many of my contemporaries, as well as myself, were baptised in a church. Our parents tried to implant a belief in God in us.

At school, on the other hand, the teachers' efforts were directed towards countering such beliefs. Every boy had to join the organisation of Pioneers, and, later, the "glorious" Leninist Komsomol or Communist Union of Youth. Pioneers and the Komsomol members are educated in the spirit of devotion to the Communist Party of the Soviet Union. Religion and belief in God are rejected completely. It is strictly forbidden to visit a church, and woe to the one who visited a church, if this became known at the school. He was publicly mocked. The teachers tried to humble him in every way possible, and life became unbearable for him. At school assemblies, he was brought forward in front of everyone and described as the worst pupil. And none of us dared to come forward in his defence. All of us remained either in cowardly silence, or even stepped forward to speak against him. It was something akin to lynching negroes.

This was the way in which the "human" Communist educational system started, the beginning of fear and cowardice in front of a friend. If any one of us believed in God, he never spoke about it with anyone for fear of being disgraced and laughed at. And this applied to me; I, too, was afraid. I was a Pioneer and before passing out of the school became a member of the Communist Union of Youth. Failure to follow this course would have closed all doors to me in further education. After leaving school, my parents wanted me to enter an institute for higher studies, but I had my own plans. I decided to study at a school for officers. The romance of military life attracted me. It seemed to me then at the age of 17 that the profession of an officer was a truly masculine one, full of danger and adventure.

So in August 1962, after passing entrance examinations, I became a cadet at the officers' school at Ryazan, where officers for airborne troops were trained.. I was to stay at that school for four years during which period we were to be made into *real* officers.

We were given intensive and comprehensive training. The programme included military and general educational subjects. Besides higher mathematics, foreign languages, physics, we studied various kinds of weapons, home and foreign, shooting, jumping with a parachute, topography, demolition work, sabotage operations and many other activities. Particular attention was paid to physical training.

We were indoctrinated intensively in the spirit of loyalty to Communism and enmity towards its enemies. The education proceeded under the slogan: "Para (Desantnik)—be prepared to sacrifice yourself in the name of your *Socialist* Motherland." This slogan was written up in letters metres high on the wall of the school's club. They tried to turn us into a suicide kind of *kamikaze*. We were prepared to do anything. In operations behind the enemy's lines, we were to act decisively and ruthlessly. Without hesitating we were to resort to terrorism, sabotage and the killing of peaceful citizens. Anything was permitted. "It is only in this way that a Para (Desantnik) can fulfil his task and achieve success" we were told by our instructors, who set out to give us a feeling of superiority over other mortals.

To emphasise this hardline approach, strict discipline prevailed. For the slightest infringement, severe punishment was meted out. It was enough to light a cigarette at the wrong moment or to appear in the street without a greatcoat, to be put under arrest for three days. I recall one occasion when we were loading equipment to go to a specially equipped camp for field firing and training in sabotage operations. We went regularly for several weeks to a site in a forest 60 km from Ryazan. Our sleeping quarters were on the third floor of the building. Six cadets were detailed to carry down mattresses, tied together in fives, and load them onto a lorry. Instead of carrying them downstairs, they started to throw the mattresses out of the window. Our platoon commander, senior Lieutenant Vilkov, was standing below, and after the first batch was thrown from the third floor, he roared: "Stop this outrage." The cadets either did not hear him or pretended not to hear, and the mattresses continued to fly down. This made Vilkov wild and he shouted something loudly. I stood nearby and laughed uproariously. Suddenly he turned towards me, pointed a finger and cried: "Five days arrest for you." "For what?" I asked. "For malicious laughter."

While at the school, I not only swotted at the various subjects, but learned to understand life. On the one hand, I was subjected to incessant inculcation of Communist ideas, and on the other, life often demonstrated the injustices of Soviet society. Several events made a particularly strong impression on me. I was a cadet at the school during the period that Khruschev was in power, or to be more accurate, during the last few years of his rule. During this time the "wise" policy of Khruschev led to a shortage of food in the USSR. There was practically no meat, butter or white bread, and people had to stand for several hours in a queue for brown bread.

We future officers did not feel these shortages to any extent and were as usual fed excellently. But the population, the workers, suffered greatly. We heard rumours of protests on the part of workers, but this was remote from our life as cadets and none of us gave any serious thought to them until one evening we were put on a state of alert. We were formed up; ordered to take our sub-machine guns; issued with 60 rounds each and told: "At one of the works in the town of Ryazan a large group of hooligans has assembled and is disturbing the social order. If the Militia cannot cope with them, we will proceed to the seat of trouble to restore law and order."

We were ordered to remain in barracks and await further orders. About two hours later, the alert order was cancelled and we continued our training in the routine way. It was only later that it became known to us, through cadets whose parents lived in Ryazan, that there were no hooligans whatever at those works, but that there had been a strike by workers, who had demanded bread. It was against *them* that we were to take action with weapons in our hands.

That was when I began to think: "How was it and why, that in a workers' and peasants' state, where, according to the Communists, power belongs to the people, we were to be sent against those very people." I was probably not the only one to have such thoughts, but we all remained silent, some out of fear, others simply because they did not want to pay any attention to it: all, with one exception.

Soon after these events, a revealing incident occurred at one of the education sessions on the history of the Communist Party of the Soviet Union (CPSU). The lecturer, Major Yakushenko, spoke to us about the enormous services that the Communist Party had rendered to the Soviet people; about how well and happily the people lived. After the lecture, he asked, as usual, whether anyone had any questions or whether anything was unclear. As a rule, no questions were put from our side on this "very interesting subject". All of us were in a hurry to leave the lecture room to make the fullest use of the break between lessons. But this time, it was different.

One of our comrades, Anatoli Sinitski, surprised us all. He was a strong chap, of small stature, who had arrived at the school from a distant village in Belorussia, with the commonsense of a peasant, and who seldom spoke up. And it was this unlikely youngster who stood up in the middle of the lecture room and, in dead silence, put the following question to the lecturer: "Well, you say that our people are living very well; then why is it that workers go on strike?" His question probably came as more of a surprise to the lecturer than to us. For a few moments, the lecturer stood in silence, evidently thinking over how he should reply to such a clearly un-Soviet question. We, too, remained silent, startled by our colleague's boldness because questioning of the official line could lead to him being expelled from the school and sent to serve in the army as a private for three years.

Sinitski did not show up at the next lecture, and we saw him again only during the evening meal in the cadets' dining room. He looked gloomy and did not want to talk to anyone.

On the same day, in the evening, our company, which included Sinitski, was assembled in one of the lecture rooms and the secretary of the Party committee in the school appeared. His speech was very short and went roughly as follows: "Comrades cadets. It is unpleasant for me to have to say this, but among you is a person who has incorrect un-Komsomol, views on life. You know about whom I am speaking. I consider that there is no place for him in the Komsomol. So, this week at the Komsomol meeting you must immediately expel Sinitski from the Komsomol."

That is what would have happened to Sinitski; he would have been thrown out of the Komsomol, and then out of the school, if other events had not taken place. On the day after that incident, 4 October 1964, an official announcement broadcast throughout the Soviet Union told of the removal of Khruschev from all his posts. His errors in the management of the state were enumerated; and, of course, all the failures of the USSR, the difficulties over foodstuffs, were laid at his door. The Party, as always, was blameless. His successor, Brezhnev, was also blameless, although he was chairman of the Presidium of the Supreme Soviet of the USSR and for a long time had sung Khruschev's praises.

After that "Kremlin revolution", they began to explain Khruschev's mistakes strenuously to us; to describe him as a man who lacked the qualities to manage the state, and so forth. The Sinitski incident was forgotten, for it turned out that he had spoken the truth. Sinitski had been saved. For us, this incident illustrated the hypocrisy of our idealist tutors, and for some of us, perhaps, the hypocrisy of the whole Soviet system.

Undoubtedly hypocrisy. What other word could be used for giving a name to the sharp switch, in one day, in the line taken by the propaganda machine? It was only yesterday that it was being impressed on us cadets that Khruschev was an outstanding man, and today it turned out that he was a completely useless administrator, who had an incorrect understanding of the problems of building up Communism.

The period Khruschev was in power was in general an unsual one. He was fond of appearing on radio and television with lengthy orations to the people. He spoke of the astonishing successes in the country's development, of the imminence of a great era of Communism and about the Soviet Union overtaking the United States very shortly, the conditions of life for the people becoming much better than in America.

To these assertions, the people gave an answer in their own way. Many jokes circulated about comparisons between conditions of life in the USSR and the USA. Here is just one of them. A delegation of Soviet workers visited the USA; an American worker, John, invited a Soviet worker, Ivan, to his home and showed him how he lived. "This," said John to Ivan, "is my little house. Here is the sitting-room for receiving guests, the nursery, the dining-room. Here is my bedroom, where I occasionally greet my mistress, and there is the bedroom of my wife, where, in my absence she may perhaps receive her lover. And now, tell me Ivan, how do you live in your Russia?" Ivan does not think for long, remembering the room in the communal flat in which he lives with his wife and two children and answers: "You know, John, I have everything you have, only without partitions."

It was in this way that life gradually showed me the enormous differences between the boastful propaganda of Communism and reality. Doubts about the justice of Communism grew in me. However, in one's youth one often lacks time to ponder deeply about life. We strive to advance. That was the way it was with me. After training for four years, I passed out of the school successfully and in my 21st year got the golden epaulettes of a lieutenant. Naturally, I was pleased. And why not, aged 21—an officer. I was posted to Kaunas, to an intelligence sub-unit of an airborne division. My independent life had begun.

In the armed forces, I saw for the first time with my own eyes what it was like to be a simple soldier in the Soviet army, his miserable existence. The general discipline and conditions of life for a private were in great contrast to those of a private in the Western armies. During their service, Soviet privates live all the time in barracks. They are strictly forbidden to leave the location of their unit. In their sleeping-quarters about 60 to 80 men are accommodated together. Each day a private is allotted duties to the last minute. Most of the time he spends on parade. Immediately after reveille, he has to fall-in for physical exercise, after that washing, then he marches in formation to the mess-hall and back. After that, he falls-in for training, which continues for six hours. Then for the midday meal, he again marches in formation, after which he is formed-up again for further exercises. In the evening, he is marched in strict formation to supper and back. And before going to his sleeping quarters, he falls-in for the evening roll-call. Sundays and other rest days differ from ordinary days in that instead of training, sporting competitions are held and in the evening artistic films are shown.

On a Saturday or Sunday only about 15 per cent of privates get permission to visit the town or village near the unit for a few hours. Leave to visit families is granted only to a few, the best of the best, and, of course, to those whose families have suffered a serious misfortune. The rest, from the beginning to the end of their service, have no possibility of visiting relatives.

The private gets three roubles 80 kop. a month, with which he has to buy bootpolish, a toothbrush and toothpaste, shaving gear and, for those who smoke, cigarettes. Soldiers are strictly forbidden to drink spirits, or even beer.

Despite all this, the private soldier is constantly assured that the conditions of his service are some of the best in the world, and that all the difficulties which he encounters are the fault of Capitalists, as they constantly threaten the Soviet Union with war.

All this made a very sombre impression on me as a youthful officer.

"Again injustice and lies," I thought. This applied not only to privates, but to officers as well. For we, too, were brought up in the spirit of enmity towards the Western nations, which were always portrayed as instigators of another world war. The injustices of the régime in the conditions prevalent in the army were still more evident.

All that was said by the government, by the Politburo, the Higher Command, political officers, was correct and just; everything that did not suit the Soviet régime was lies: the consequences of Capitalism and ideological deviation. Towards the end of the first year of my service as an officer, nothing was left of my youthful dreams about the integrity and manliness of the profession of an army officer. In reality, everything looked different. One often had to act in a way contrary to one's convictions and conscience. "Less thought, more discipline" was the daily command. The authority of an order was paramount; the one who had more stars on his epaulettes was always right.

Such a way of life did not suit me and I decided to leave the army. But how to do this? A Soviet officer cannot leave the army just like that; he is obliged to serve for 25 years. I was aware of only two ways in which individual young officers managed to get out. The first way is an illness, so serious than an officer is considered to be unfit for further service.

The alternative is more complicated. The officer starts to commit breaches of discipline systematically; to turn up late for duty and to drink too much. After headquarters become fully convinced of his incorrigibility, the officer is expelled publicly from the army with a bad report, making it difficult for him to start a normal life as a civilian.

Both courses seemed unacceptable to me; the first because I was not ill; the second because it was lengthy (sometimes it took years) and involved many unpleasantnesses. I cannot say now what I would have done to get out of the army had I not been helped by one event. One day several of us young officers were sitting having dinner in one of the coffee houses in the town of Kaunas and talking about service in the army, about mutual acquaintances and general inconsequential matters.

Suddenly the conversation brought out a point that proved to be very important for me and, in the end played a significant rôle in my life. One of the officers, Vladimir Gushchin, related what had occurred in the case of a friend whom he had met recently. "Do you know where he is working now?" he asked us in an awed voice, and went on to provide the answer: "He is now an officer in the KGB." "How did he manage that?" he was asked, one cannot leave the army just like that. "It's different in the case of the KGB," replied

Gauschin, "the KGB can arrange anything." The officers continued talking while I sat and thought: "Why shouldn't I try somehow to get a job in the KGB? This would free me from the army." The thought continued to trouble me for a long time.

At the time, I knew very little about the KGB. I had heard that it was engaged in intelligence and fighting the enemies of the state, and that was about as far as my knowledge extended. In the USSR, there is almost no talk about that organisation, and if anyone speaks of it, it is with fear. This applies to army officers too, as the power of the KGB extends not only to the civilian population but also to the army.

Yes, I had something to think about. By that time, my belief in my country, the "most just and happy state in the world", had been somewhat undermined. I had been shaken by many falsehooods and other negative aspects of the Communist régime. The KGB was an organisation which defended and protected that régime, and I was faced with having to make a decision about joining it. Various factors played their part. The main one was that at the time I was not yet completely disillusioned with the régime. I still had some kind of faith in the idea of Communism. Naturally intelligence attracted me by its secrecy. Moreover, joining the KGB freed me from the army. I decided to enter that service.

The next problem was how to achieve that objective. The KGB is vitally concerned about the reliability of its personnel. Only the most reliable and convinced Soviet citizens—who must be Communists—manage to get accepted. Moreover, the KGB itself finds suitable individuals for service in it. No one was aware of my doubts about the justice of Communism, so I could get through a check on my reliability. It was true that I was not a Communist, but this problem could be solved. I could become a member of the CPSU any time, all the more so, as I had received several suggestions to this effect from the secretary of the unit's Party organisation, which I had turned down all the time on the grounds of my youthfulness. So, in my view I was a suitable candidate. Yet years might elapse if I waited until the KGB noticed me, if ever.

I decided to take action in accordance with the principle: "If the mountain will not come to Mohammed, then Mohammed must go to the mountain." I went to the Special Section of the KGB for the Guards Airborne Division in which I was serving, and asked to be taken to the chief of this section, Lieutenant-Colonel Bloshchup. He received me politely and expressed interest in why I had turned up. I told him immediately of my wish to work in an organisation concerned with state security, and made every effort to make my request appear as convincing as possible. I said that work in intelligence and counter-intelligence was my life's dream. I emphasised the necessity and significance of such work for the state, and so on.

Evidently I made a favourable impression. The colonel's face expressed satisfaction, almost pride. It looked as though he had not heard such praises of the KGB for a long time. He questioned me closely about my relatives, about myself, wrote something in his notebook and said that I would get a more definite answer in a week's time.

Exactly a week later, I was sitting once more in the same room. This time it was the colonel who did most of the talking. He told me that during the week the KGB had collected detailed testimonials and other references about me. All these were satisfactory, so that the probability of my being able to join up was not excluded, but this would become possible only after a careful vetting of me and my relatives.

The interview raised my hopes; all that remained was that I should pass the family screening. This took about three months, and during that time I had occasion to meet various KGB men; to talk to them and to answer thousands of different questions. My capabilities and qualities, the level of my general training and, of course, my knowledge of Marxism-Leninsm, were tested. Besides that, I had to go before a strict medical commission.

At last, everything seemed to be over. At the beginning of December, I was summoned by Colonel Bloshchup, who congratulated me on having passed through the vetting successfully, but added that it was still premature for me to rejoice. I had to have an interview with the chief of the Special Section of the KGB of the Baltic Military District, Major-General Deev, who would convey the final decision to me.

This interview took place about 10 December. General Deev was a thickset man, of medium height, aged about 50, with piercing eyes which looked at me attentively. My conversation with him was short and general. I presented myself smartly: "Comrade General, Lieutenant Myaghov reporting to you in accordance with your orders."

"Sit down," he barked. I sat gingerly on the edge of the chair, and waited. The general remained silent, trying only to sum me up for about three minutes. Suddenly breaking the silence, he asked loudly: "What is your opinion of yourself?"

What a difficult question, I thought, but answered immediately: "High, comrade General." "You all have high opinions of yourselves and then work badly," he growled. "Do you drink vodka?" "No, no," I cried.

"At first all declare that they do not drink, and then later somehow turn out to be alcoholics. Do you read books, have you a knowledge of literature?"—"Yes, certainly, comrade General."

"Well, tell me who was the laureate this year of the Lenin award for literature?" asked the general.

"Who the hell knows?" I thought. Now I am lost. But I mentioned some name as a guess. The general himself evidently did not know the answer, for he remained satisfied with my reply and even rated the diversity of my knowledge highly.

Finally he informed me that the question of my admittance to the KGB was settled favourably; congratulated me on such an important event and said: "Await the order from Andropov about your inclusion in the service of agencies of the KGB."

What an interview, I thought later; a few bad questions and all is over. It was in that way that my work in the KGB began.

CHAPTER 3

The Politburo's army of spies

A NUMBER of books and articles have already given a detailed account of the structure of the Committee of State Security, its component parts, its chief directorates and departments. I want to deal with its ramifications from the viewpoint of its creators and of those whom it serves, the Politburo and the Soviet Government. The KGB's role not only in espionage, but in monitoring all activities throughout the Soviet bloc, and in penetrating and influencing Western organisations—and even foreign policy—is clearly shown in copies of top secret documents I brought with me to the West. See Appendices I, II and III.

What is the KGB? I will try to depict it from within.

After the October Revolution, the Bolshevik faction of the Communist Party, led by Lenin, came to power. However, the struggle for power in Russia did not end at that point: instead it became more bitter and bloody and fratricidal civil war began.

During that period, the survival of the Communist Bolshevik cause was at stake. This drove the Party to wage war without pity or scruple, using armed detachments of workers and soldiers (from which the Red Army was later built up) which physically annihilated the opponents of Soviet power. Party agitators and the press were used to condition the popular masses.

On 20 December 1917, the Bolsheviks established the so-called "Cheka" (Special Commission) to combat "counter-revolutionary and other criminal elements". The Cheka was headed by Dzerzhinski ("Iron Felix"). It became the secret police of the Bolshevik régime. Its members, the "Chekists", were given extensive powers which they used to fight counter-revolutionary elements, and use them they did. Human life had little meaning for them, as for instance during the so-called "Red Terror" when the enemies of the Soviet Government, numbering among them many small traders selling matches or cigarettes on the street were executed by the Chekists at the scene of their "crimes".

The ferociousness of the Cheka quickly became known throughout the country and the very word "Chekist" was enough to strike terror into the hearts of many.

The Civil War ended with the victory of the Bolsheviks and peace returned for everyone but the Cheka, which continued its internal war against the enemies of Communism. During the years since the Bolshevik régime came to power, the Cheka has developed from a small organisation into the huge secret service of the Soviet Government which has annhilated some 20 million innocent Soviet citizens in its prisons and forced labour camps.

This secret service has had many names, Cheka, GPU, NKVD, MGB. At present, it is called the KGB, the Committee of State Security. What is the KGB today?

In a Top Secret manual for training KGB workers, *Legal Statute of the Organs of the USSR KGB* (the author is named as Lunev), it is stated: " . . . the KGB is a political working organisation of the CPSU. The KGB and its local organs carry out their work on the basis of the fulfilment of party directives and of the laws, decrees and instructions of the government . . . All important questions relative to KGB activity are previously decided by the Central Committee of the CPSU and are enforced by KGB orders . . . "

Thus it is a component part of the Soviet Communist Party, in fact, its armed or fighting wing. This huge organisation, employing approximately 110,000 officials, is simultaneously responsible for espionage, counter-espionage and the functions of a secret political police force. For this work it is endowed with great power, extending not only over Soviet citizens but also, to some extent, over the citizens of other Communist states. In fulfilling the will of the Politburo and Soviet government, the KGB exerts an influence on many important world events.

The law setting out its basic tasks is the *Statute of the Committee of State Security attached to the Council of Ministers of the USSR.* This top secret document remains to this day the basis of the whole organisation.

Duties of KGB organs:

1. To carry out espionage work in Capitalist countries
— to ensure that agents penetrate the state, political, scientific, technical and espionage centres of imperialist states
— to penetrate the headquarters of international Capitalist organisations with the aim of aggravating contradictions and difficulties occurring in their activities.
— to obtain reliable information revealing the political and strategic military plans of the enemy and its espionage agencies
— to supply documentary information on the latest scientific technical achievements
— to implant agents in émigré organisations abroad and work towards their disintegration and ideological destruction
— to give the enemy misinformation for political and operational

purposes

2. To carry out counter-espionage work actively and aggressively, at the same time penetrating enemy espionage organs

— to find and work upon persons suspected of belonging to imperialist espionage agencies; stop the activities of foreign espionage officials and their agents

— KGB organs operate among the population, in the Soviet army and navy, in frontier and internal troop detachments and at other special and particularly important points

— they ensure the security of state and military secrets and organise counter-espionage measures to protect Soviet citizens abroad from the endeavours of imperialist espionage agencies, as well as forestalling any betrayal of the Motherland

— they carry out counter-espionage and espionage activities against imperialist state embassies

3. They are obliged to struggle against anti-Soviet and nationalist elements

— they seek out state criminals, authors and distributors of anti-Soviet documents

— they work against church officials and members of religious sects

— they prevent undesirable links between the Catholic Church and the Vatican

4. They make up the bodyguards of Party leaders (Members and Candidate Members of the CC CPSU Politburo) and Government leaders

— to ensure and organise governmental communications, operate radio counter-espionage services as well as keeping account of all working radio stations in the country at large

5. To defend the frontiers of the USSR (KGB frontier troops)

6. KGB organs carry out individual tasks entrusted to them by the Central Committee of the CPSU and Soviet Government.

The KGB is thus faced with clear, concrete tasks, from influencing the course of world political events to persecuting any worker dissatisfied with his living conditions, or any innocent servant of the church.

A top secret KGB manual *Organisation of KGB Counter-Espionage Work* where, in setting out 'Espionage Activity of the KGB', it is once again emphasised that " . . . the determining factor in the espionage activity of the KGB is the foreign policy of the Soviet Government", will also be referred to. I shall not deal with well-known cases, such as Britain's expulsion of more than a hundred people, namely KGB officials engaged in espionage or other subversive activities, from the Soviet Embassy in London, or the discovery in Belgium of a Soviet agent network. It will be more productive to look at unsensational events little-known to the general public, but nevertheless significant, showing how Soviet security organs fulfil the task of aggravating the contradictions which exist between member states of capitalist organisations and blocs.

NATO was, and remains to this day, the USSR's main enemy. For this reason Moscow has always made every effort to weaken this organisation. One such method is its policy of working for an internal split in NATO, and here France has been the main target in recent years. In carrying out this policy, the Kremlin used all its resources, working along two channels simultaneously.

One such channel was official Moscow policy. For example, there was the conclusion of agreements between the USSR and France, and the exchange of visits between heads of the two states. There were meetings between representatives of the Soviet and French governments. Thus, the Soviet Minister of Foreign Affairs, Gromyko, was in Paris from 25-30 April 1965. He met French officials for discussions on Vietnam, Cambodia, nuclear weapons and security questions.

On 15 May of the same year, Gromyko met Couve de Murville in Vienna and the latter visited the Soviet Union between 28 October and 2 November of the same year. Subjects which they discussed included the improvement of relations between their two countries, European questions and the German problem. An agreement between the Soviet Union and France was signed in Paris in 1965 on the Soviet use of the French colour television system. In November 1965, a delegation of Soviet scientists headed by Professor Sedov visited France to discuss the launching of French satellites into the earth's orbit with the help of Soviet rockets.

1966 was also a year of active negotiations between the Soviet Union and France. General de Gaulle paid an official visit to the Soviet Union between 20 June and 1 July. Peyrefitte was in the USSR from 28 September to 11 October. On 15 October, a Soviet warship began a week's visit to Toulon and the French Minister of Finance and Economic Affairs, Debré, was in the Soviet Union from 16 to 20 November to discuss long-term economic and technical collaboration between the two countries.

A series of treaties were signed between the Soviet Union and France during 1966. On 5 May, agreement on large-scale exchanges in nuclear research was reached between the Soviet Committee for the Use of Atomic Energy and the French Atomic Energy Commission. On 29 September, a protocol was signed in Paris making provision for the establishment of a Franco-Soviet Chamber of Commerce, and, on 10 October, an agreement on technical collaboration was signed between Renault-Peugeot and the Soviet Government.

Alongside all this, a campaign designed to prove an unbreakable friendship between the USSR and France was carried on by the Soviet press and radio. Newspapers and magazines published a succession of articles telling of an historic friendship spanning many years. At the same time, every effort was made to play on French national feeling by emphasising France's significance as a world power and its decisive role in Europe.

A second clandestine channel was KGB activity. Using its agents among Soviet journalists and officials of the various agencies in France, as well as among members of the Franco-Soviet Friendship Society, it propagated actively among politicians the theme that the country's political independence suffered from the fact that it was a member of NATO and that foreign troops were stationed on its territory, especially American troops. This same line of thought was canvassed by KGB agents among French citizens recruited in political circles.

On 11 March 1966, in an official note addressed to the member countries of NATO, de Gaulle announced the withdrawal of France from the North Atlantic Treaty Organisation. In accordance with Article 9 of the North Atlantic Treaty, the withdrawal of France from NATO was given final acknowledgement on 1 July 1967. These measures were received with great satisfaction in Moscow. The newspapers were full of praise for the wise peaceloving actions of the French Government. The Kremlin welcomed the very real weakening of NATO, the more so because, as Moscow hoped, other member countries might follow France's example. The KGB leaders also did not hide their satisfaction at recognition of the fact that they, too, had played their part in these events.

France's withdrawal from NATO was seized upon as an instructive example in KGB officer courses. In 1968, the head of KGB School No 311, in a lecture to future officers about the organisation's activities abroad, stated plainly that, in the opinion of the Politburo, events in France were a positive result of the efforts of the Soviet Government and of the successes of the KGB. Many people may object that other factors played their part in the Paris decision to leave NATO and to forbid the stationing of foreign troops on French territory. Be that as it may, the fact remains: in its secret deliberations, the Kremlin confirmed that the French actions reflected the correctness of Politburo and Soviet Government policies, in which they were actively helped by the KGB.

The European Economic Community (EEC) is also disliked in Moscow; it prefers a disunited and weak Europe, and the policies of the Kremlin leadership are directed towards frustrating moves towards unity. In an attempt to split the Community, Moscow has tried to conclude bilateral agreements with individual members. Just such an attempt was made with the Federal Republic of Germany in 1974.

The KGB, pursuing this policy, also selected weak EEC links like Italy and France, where Communist influence is widespread. The Soviet radio and press, weapons in the hands of the Politburo and government, have long been working in that direction. They regularly criticise EEC shortcomings, and underline the unreality of European union.

As well as work against Europe, the KGB is widely involved in measures against the Chinese. Since about 1971, the school of the First Chief Directorate of the KGB has included a special Chinese Department. Officers, who will work exclusively against China, are trained there and the Chinese Department is represented in all residencies in the Far East.

The KGB Directorate in Khabarovsk, a town on the Chinese border north of Vladivostok, has a strong Third Department which works against China. The Second Chief Directorate has cadres in KGB Provincial Directorates who are solely concerned with work against China.

Since 1971, the KGB has devoted much earnest effort to that target. China is an immediate neighbour and officially the KGB regards the situation as very serious. In 1962, when the relations between USSR and China deteriorated, the KGB was reproached by the Government because it was not in a position to explain what had changed in China, what was happening there and how the situation might develop. Since then, the KGB's main aim has been to build up a good espionage system in China to collect political and military intelligence, because at the moment it is impossible for the KGB to exercise political influence there. The acquisition of such influence is, of course, its eventual aim and the Politburo does not exclude the possibility that USSR and China may later become friends once more.

For the forseeable future, it will be impossible for the KGB itself to recruit agents in China and they must rely on the use of illegals. In Siberia, there are a large number of Chinese, who were born there and provide a ready source of recruits for the KGB. Also, the KGB, under false colours, is actively recruiting agents in both Western and Third World countries with whom the Chinese have economic and cultural relations.

In Samarkand, there is a school for illegals which trains mostly agents from the Third World. Its students include Africans, Indians, Iranians, and Asians. Courses last up to 10 years.

Besides the establishment of agents inside China, the KGB is involved in planning measures to combat what is known as "The Chinese Penetration Army". The People's Republic of China is reported to have established an army of between two and three million men for guerilla operations against Siberia. They will operate in groups of about six men to penetrate into the hinterland and carry out sabotage attacks. In true Chinese fashion, these groups will have no transport or logistics but will be self-supporting. The KGB fear they could prove a severe problem in wartime because there will be no "front line" and Siberian roads are inadequate for large scale army operations.

One aspect of KGB work abroad is its activities in Germany, both in the Federal Republic of Germany (West Germany) and the German Democratic Republic (East Germany). Having spent five years on GDR territory, I am well acquainted with its work in this area. About 60 KGB departments are allocated to the task there, with no less than 1,500 KGB agents. The operatives enjoy almost as many rights in East Germany as on Soviet territory, with the exception that they cannot arrest East German citizens. This task is undertaken by the Ministry of State Security, or MfS, of the GDR. The KGB voluntarily divested itself of this privilege in order to demonstrate its respect, if only outwardly, for the so-called independent East German state. In all other respects, no deference whatever is shown to East German sovereignty. The KGB has the right to use East Germans as agents as a means of political control of the citizens; to use them for espionage and counter-espionage purposes; to evaluate their political reliability and in many cases to decide their fate. It makes full use of the MfS and of the police and, in fact, often gives them orders. All this is done with the knowledge and approval of the GDR government; not a vestige is left of its independence. Among themselves, KGB officers refer to the GDR as the 16th Republic of the USSR.

KGB agents sent to the GDR belong basically in two Directorates. The First Chief Directorate of the KGB has about 900 people, whose main task is espionage abroad. The Third Chief Directorate has about 600 people and their main task is the security of the Group of Soviet Forces in Germany as well as counter-espionage directed against West Germany and against American, British and French espionage agencies. Of the Third Directorate workers, about 150 are concerned solely with espionage.

About 1,200 of all KGB workers in the GDR are engaged in espionage activities directed mainly against the FRG as well as against American, British and French troops stationed in West Germany and in the Western Sector of Berlin. To carry out these activities and to get information about the enemy, agents are needed in the enemy camp. Various categories are recruited.

A small number of agents are recruited from GDR citizens who are entitled to visit West Germany periodically. As a rule, they are observation agents, i.e. they collect information of interest to the KGB by means of visual observation. The method works as follows: GDR resident KGB agent, Schultze, is given permission to visit relations in town N in the FRG. The KGB knows that an American radio unit is stationed there, so Schultze is given the task of getting close to it while visiting his relations, and noting the numbers of military vehicles; making a plan of the military emplacement and if possible photographing it. Having obtained this information, the KGB analyses what changes have taken place at the enemy encampment. Has any new equipment or armament appeared? Has the number of soldiers been increased?

In addition, KGB agents among the citizens are used to obtain tip-offs. That is to say while they are in West Germany, they collect details of the characters of FRG citizens or American, British and French servicemen who occupy important posts, be it in state organisations, the army, espionage circles or in important industrial and other enterprises, whom the KGB can recruit as agents at some future date.

KGB men recruit most of the agents intended for collecting information about the enemy from among visiting West Germans. In these operations, the KGB is "at home" on its own territory where it enjoys full power, and this, in turn, creates favourable conditions. Such recruitment is not a hurried affair, but is carried out after careful preparation, and is almost always successful.

All FRG citizens who visit East Germany are recorded in the GDR MfS and police files, while 90 per cent of them are also recorded in KGB indexes. For every visitor from the FRG or any other capitalist country (the KGB groups them all together as Westerners), one or another department makes out a special card. This card notes all the visitor's relations in both Germanys, information on where he and his relatives work and whether he or his relatives have access to secret material.

If the KGB agent comes to the conclusion that a Westerner by virtue of his official position or personal qualities is suitable, he begins preparations for recruitment. This follows different patterns, the Westerner either agrees to co-operate with the KGB for money, or he is compelled to work for them by threat and blackmail. Sometimes a beautfiul woman (or alternatively a handsome man) is employed. There are, of course, the rare exceptions, where a Westerner co-operates out of political conviction. It is an amazing fact that the majority of recruitments of FRG and other Western citizens are concluded successfully on GDR territory. In all probability the fact that the victims have no way out plays an important role.

If, when someone is being recruited, neither conviction, money nor

blackmail helps, then the KGB employs direct threats. The Westerner
is told that if he refuses to co-operate, he will be accused of espionage
or other "subversive" activity against Soviet troops or against the
GDR, that he will be sentenced and put in gaol. This is not difficult
under "socialist law" as there is no trouble in finding witnesses and
proof. Sometimes, his relatives living in the GDR are threatened.
Subjected to pressure of this kind, the victim agrees to collaborate.
Many people will say that having been recruited in this way, he can
contact the appropriate authority when he returns to the FGR and
tell them what has happened. The KGB officers do not overlook this
possibility; they compel the recruit to sign a statement about his
"voluntary" agreement to collaborate with the KGB which is dated
some two years before the actual event. This trick, as well as the
threats aimed at relatives, cut off all escape for the reluctant new
agent. In time, he gets accustomed to his position, the more so
because his connection with the KGB brings him in money, and,
therefore, he continues to collaborate.

KGB officers also recruit agents directly on FGR territory, travelling
to Western Germany as journalists, trade representatives or in other
guises. They are particularly active in West Berlin, exploiting its status
of "a free town". Here the KGB feel quite at home; recruit agents;
arrange meetings with agents in "safe" flats; organise; bug telephone
conversations and carry on external observations. Not for nothing
did I emphasise the danger of my stay in West Berlin when describing
my flight to the West.

The 400 KGB officers responsible for counter-espionage on GDR
territory are kept busy, not only among the troops and other Soviet
citizens but among East Germans, recruiting agents and hunting spies,
"anti-socialists" and other enemies.

Assessing the results of 1,500 KGB officers' work in the GDR the
following picture emerges: about 2,000 agents from among FRG
citizens recruited and collaborating; 1,500 agents from GDR citizens;
and about 4,000 agents from among Soviet troops or citizens. Besides
the KGB officers in the GDR, collaborators also work against the
FRG, working there under the cover of the Soviet embassy or of
agency offices. It should not be forgotten that MfS works actively
against the FRG, which it considers the main target. Espionage
agencies of other East European countries do not lag far behind. To
sum up the effort of all Eastern espionage systems in West Germany,
the total of FRG citizens working for these espionage agencies can
be put at about 8,000.

It was my lot to work on GDR territory from the beginning of
1969 to the beginning of 1974, that is to say, precisely at the time
when it seemed that a new period of friendship and co-operation was

beginning between the Soviet Union and the Federal Republic. It seemed at the time that this would have a great positive effect for these two countries, and would also help the whole political atmosphere in Europe and serve as a spur to better East-West relations.

In 1969, a treaty was being prepared between the leaders of the FRG and USSR relating to rejection of the use of force and mutual peaceful co-operation between states. These preparations were particularly active in the first half of 1970. From 30 January to 22 May of that year, FRG State Secretary Egon Bahr and Foreign Minister of the USSR Gromyko were particularly concerned with these questions. They met each other at frequent intervals and the preparatory work was successfully completed. Real possibilities were found for the conclusion of a treaty.

During these meetings, there was much talk of the possibility of reducing tension between the two countries, of demonstrating friendly intentions and mutual trust. Officially everything looked good. At that very time, KGB Chairman Andropov, with the approval and consent of the Politburo and the Soviet Government, issued Top Secret KGB order No 0039 of 28 April 1970, requiring **KGB** workers:

— to make decisive efforts to recruit agents in the FRG
— to make more active use of double-agent recruitment among agents discovered as belonging to FRG agencies
— to organise active work among FRG citizens presenting an operational interest.

This order was received at a time when Moscow was sure of concluding a treaty. The Kremlin also knew of the Bonn Government's intention to improve its relations with Poland, the GDR and with other European Communist states, and was counting on the possibility of improving the political atmosphere in Europe. Nevertheless, the Soviet Government and Politburo viewed this whole process as a temporary manifestation and tried to extract from it the maximum gain.

The treaty rejecting the use of force and mutual co-operation between the FRG and the USSR was signed on 12 August 1970. The following November, the FRG concluded a treaty with the People's Republic of Poland (PRP) recognising the Oder-Neisse line as the Western frontier of Poland and bilaterally rejecting the use of force.

Many leading world politicians began to speak of the goodwill of the Soviet leadership and of a forthcoming basic improvement in relations between East and West. But for the KGB, the lessening of tension meant an increase in their activities in Europe. Particularly exacting tasks were placed before those KGB workers who found themselves in the GDR. The central KGB apparat gave them the task of achieving a more active and many-sided exploitation of the new possibilities, as a result of the improved relations between the two German states. It demanded that they create a greatly expanded agent network in the FRG.

At the end of 1972, a treaty was concluded between the FRG and the GDR regulating their relationship. One of the results was that FRG citizens had more opportunities of visiting the GDR, and this immediately attracted the attention of the KGB leadership. In a few months, the staff in the GDR received an order from the KGB chairman—No 0042 of 8 May 1973—pointing out that this was a period of great responsibility for them: they were to expand activities in all directions, and were particularly ordered to exploit the increased number of visits by FRG citizens. Such actions, approved by the Politburo and government, prove that the Soviet leadership did not really want improved relations at all with the West; some of the concessions were made solely to obtain the maximum gain on the political front in the future.

CHAPTER 4

The Soviet "Mafia's" network of fear

THE KGB organs, in fulfilling the role of a secret political police force to combat anti-Soviet, nationalist and other hostile elements in "the most just and democratic country in the world", are endowed with such power as to nullify completely the significance of the much-lauded Soviet Constitution—still, incidentally, in its Stalinist form—and of other laws.

In the top secret document entitled *Statute of the Committee for State Security attached to the Council of Ministers of the USSR* quoted earlier, it is stated

" . . . to fulfil the tasks set before them, KGB organs are endowed with general and special powers."

Special Powers

KGB organs have the right:

1. To carry on operational work with agents; to maintain a network of agents; to maintain "safe" and local reporting flats; to organise eavesdropping activities and to undertake secret photography.

2. To organise and carry out secret observation and to maintain agents.

3. To take special measures to curtail criminal activity. To set up secret control over both international and internal postal and telegraphic communications. To employ operational printing equipment in order to fabricate "cover" documents.

4. To check up on the behaviour of persons who have served sentences for particularly dangerous crimes against the state.

5. To check on the coding service, on secret communications and on security in all ministries and other official organisations, as well as in organisations subordinate to the KGB itself.

6. To carry out investigatory work on state and other crimes which fall within their competence; to detain or arrest suspected persons, to make searches, confiscations etc.

7. To check documents of foreigners and Soviet citizens crossing USSR frontiers, to check on all printed matter carried and also on all loads transported either as hand luggage or ordinary luggage. To check that all foreigners leave USSR territory at the appointed time and to check on foreign personnel employed in all means of transport.

31

KGB organs, being organs of state administration, are also endowed with general powers

1. To publish obligatory state regulations and check on fulfilment of them.

2. To safeguard state secrets and limit the number of persons permitted to work on secret documents.

3. To sanction the movement of foreigners into and out of USSR territory.

4. To maintain working relations with and provide help to other organisations of state administration.

5. To carry out preliminary checks and decide whether to issue permits or not for entry into or exit from the USSR.

6. To decide on questions relative to assumption, leaving or deprivation of Soviet citizenship. . . .

As this document demonstrates, practically nothing is beyond the scope of the KGB on Soviet territory. Other top secret KGB documents add to the list of rights granted to Chekists by the Politburo and Soviet Government. For example, *Statute of the Committee for State Security attached to the Council of Ministers of the USSR* states that KGB organs have the right to control international and internal postal and telegraphic communications (while at the same time the Soviet Constitution guarantees secrecy of correspondence). To carry out this surveillance, the PK service (abbreviated form of Russian *Perlyustratsiya Korespondentsii*—Secret Censoring of Letters) attached to the Operational-Technical Directorate (OTU) of the KGB was formed. Workers belonging to this service are attached to every Oblast Directorate of the KGB and to other KGB departments of similar rank. They work at Oblast and other central post offices. They are disguised as ordinary postal workers, occupy specially separated rooms and maintain a daily check on all letters and telegrams which arrive. Total coverage is impossible, but spot checks are made based on the tasks set by order of the KGB leadership. In the top secret manual *Fundamentals of Counter-Espionage Activities of KGB Organs*—by Bannikov, it is stated that the PK service has the following tasks:

1. To set aside, on instructions of operational KGB departments, the international and internal correspondence of persons of interest to KGB organs.

2. To discover the agents of foreign espionage organisations, state criminals and authors of anonymous anti-Soviet documents by means of comparison of handwriting used in correspondence.

3. To keep a check on everything despatched abroad and a record of all persons carrying on a correspondence with capitalist countries.

4. To check postal despatches for the presence of secret writing and other forms of conspiratorial communication.

5. To keep a check on the internal correspondence from persons working and residing in areas where special security regulations are in force.

6. To carry out instructions of operational departments when collecting correspondence from post boxes, in handing over individual documents and in establishing addresses when handing over correspondence addressed to post box numbers as well as assisting KGB organs in taking legal action over documents which provide evidence of hostile activities.

7. To set aside documents based solely on external indications.

These same tasks are specially mentioned in the order No 00220 issued by the Chairman of the KGB in 1964 which *inter alia* demanded yet again ever greater use of all possibilities open to PK service. In practice, this means that the personal letters of any Soviet citizen may be, and frequently are, secretly checked by the KGB. Besides opening personal correspondence, the Operational-Techincal Directorate checks on telephone conversations; organises and carries out eavesdropping operations on persons of interest to the KGB and carries out secret searches.

To fulfil the required secret observational work or shadowing of both Soviet citizens and visiting foreigners, there is attached to the Seventh Directorate of the KGB the so-called "NN" Service (External Observation Service) which is, in fact, entitled to shadow practically everyone.

The same manual, *Fundamentals of Counter-Espionage Activities of KGB Organs,* states:

" . . . the following are objects of external scrutiny by NN Service: "

1. Foreigners suspected of hostile activity: diplomats and officials of other representational offices, tourists, merchant seamen, students, press, radio and television correspondents, members of delegations and all foreigners visiting on private business.

2. All persons in the process of being scrutinised and checked by the KGB.

3. Criminals proved to be guilty, but not yet arrested.

4. Relations and friends of state criminals sought by the KGB.

5. All other persons whom the KGB considers it necessary to keep under observation in the interests of the security of the state.

One type of activity is secret observation of persons considered by the KGB to be a potential danger to the state. These include people who have served a sentence for some so-called state crime: be it "slander on the Soviet social and state system" or "anti-Soviet propaganda and agitation". The KGB has to check on all such persons as well as on some other citizens. In Chekist parlance such control is called operational observation, and is organised with the help of KGB agents, PK and NN services and other agencies.

KGB Chairman's order No 0080 of 1965 says:

" . . . Operational observation—secret scrutiny of those persons who have served sentences for particularly dangerous crimes against the state and also scrutiny of all persons, who because of their past activities, present a danger for the Soviet state. Categories of persons subject to operational observation:

"1. Former agents or officials of capitalist states who have served sentences or who have been proved guilty though not made to serve sentences who, because of the possibilities before them may be of interest to the enemy.

"2. Former leaders and active participants of anti-Soviet nationalist organisations during the Great Patriotic War.

"3. Former leaders and active participants of nationalist underground movements.

"4. Former leaders of anti-Soviet organisations in the post-war period.

"5. Persons who occupied positions of command in the Russian Liberation Army.

"6. Persons who have served sentences for betrayal of their country or for attempted betrayal during the post-war period.

"7. Defectors from capitalist countries resident in the USSR.

"8. Former members of bourgeois governments.

"9. Heads and prominent members of church organisations and sects whose ideology is anti-Soviet.

"10. Former members of foreign anti-Soviet organisations, Trotskyists, Zionists."

The order ends:

"The aim of operational observation, the possible revelation of efforts by the person under observation to renew his hostile activity. Period during which observation is applicable, up to death itself."

The KGB not only carries on the struggle against so-called "internal enemies" but attempts to keep the population in a state of fear and obedience. To this end, it employs a method called "Prophylaxis". For example, some Soviet citizen, say a student called Ivanov, is interested in studying foreign literature and also takes an interest in events abroad. Sometimes, among his fellow-students, he expresses the view that not all is bad in Capitalist countries; that there are some positive factors from which one can learn. Such comment would become known to the KGB via an informer. Of course, Ivanov is not an "internal enemy", because he does not condemn Soviet power. He does not criticise the order of things but, in the opinion of the KGB, if not stopped in time, he may become an anti-Soviet. Furthermore, the principal danger is that Ivanov may have a negative effect on others. The KGB official responsible for the institute where Ivanov is studying decides to summon him for a chat. During this chat Ivanov admits (and who would not do the same?) his "incorrect behaviour" and gives his solemn assurance that it will never happen again. The official condescendingly gives him to understand that he believes him, then summons the secretary of the Komsomol organisation to which Ivanov belongs and suggest that Ivanov speak at the next meeting to confess his sins. Ivanov, of course, agrees readily for he knows that the KGB indulges in bad jokes, and he may be thrown out of the institute. So at the next Komsomol meeting the farce is played out. Ivanov makes a speech; beating his chest and admitting his mistakes. A number of his colleagues speak; condemning him and accusing him of having lost his Komsomol vigilance and so forth. But, of course, the majority of those taking part are fully aware that the cold hand of the KGB lies heavy on all. Nevertheless, most play an active part in the show, the simple reason being fear, which is exactly what the KGB wants.

The rules of this technique and the cases where it is to be applied and its documentation are all specified under the orders of the KGB Chairman, 00225 of 1959 and 00117 of 1964:

"Prophylaxis is a system embracing agents, operational work and other measures to forestall the occurrence of particularly dangerous crimes against the state as well as politically harmful anti-social acts of Soviet citizens. Actions which call for prophylaxis:

"1. Links with foreigners for speculative and general purposes which could be exploited by espionage agencies.

"2. Spreading information about one's work or official duties which is not meant to be publicised, although not a matter which concerns state or military secrets.

"3. Membership of immoral groups.

"4. Membership of sects and religious followings whose activities are forbidden by law.

"5. Incorrect interpretation of questions relative to Soviet Government and CPSU policies, in cases where the interpretation is not hostile in intent.

"6. Links with nationalists, where the links have no criminal intent.

"7. Worship of bourgeois influences."

After a Soviet citizen has been subjected to this treatment, the KGB keeps him under secret surveillance for a year, and if he repeats his mistake, he may be found guilty and deprived of his freedom for a couple of years. In addition, the KGB records his name in its special card index as being politically unreliable, which will have a permanently negative effect throughout his life.

Despite all the resources at its command, the KGB would be powerless without agents, its secret informants. Therefore, it is no accident that the *Statute of the KGB attached to the Council of Ministers of the USSR* states at the very beginning that "KGB organs have the right to carry on operational work with agents and maintain a network of agents. . . . "

Agents (the common people themselves call them *Shpiks*) produce the major portion of the KGB's information. Soviet society is riddled with agents and informers. They are recruited from all levels of society: collective farm and factory workers, students and soldiers, heads of industrial undertakings and army officers, high-ranking church dignitaries and scientists. Indeed, the whole Soviet Union is covered by a KGB net, creating an atmosphere of general mistrust and fear. Everyone suspects everyone else of being a *Shpik*. Many do not even trust their near relations. Few dare to voice their real thoughts. To operate an anti-Soviet underground organisation in such an atmosphere is well-nigh impossible. This network of spies is vital for the maintenance of the survival of the régime.

Nationalism is one of the vulnerable parts of Soviet society. Although official propaganda trumpets with all its might that the nationalist question has been finally solved, and Brezhnev, in a speech on the 50th anniversary of the formation of the USSR, stated that a new society of nations had been formed in the USSR, the people know that the reality is very different. The Communist régime has forcibly united in a single state many nationalities and national minorities. But as it was centuries ago, so it is today: Russians remain Russians, Lithuanians remain Lithuanians, the Uzbeks are Uzbeks, and Estonians, Estonians. Not a single nationality wishes to disappear without trace. Many, like the Lithuanians, Estonians and Latvians, are at present actively engaged in the struggle against Russification. For some, the question is even more serious, for they are struggling for their very existence. These include the Crimean Tartars who were forcibly expelled from their native region 30 years ago; sent to the bare Kazakh steppe and still have no right to return to their original homeland. And that is not all, for the Soviet leadership pretends that neither the Tartars nor any problems connected with them even exist.

In spite of all the pressures, the struggle for national independence still goes on. For this reason, one of the KGB's main tasks, both internally and abroad, is to fight nationalist elements. Conscious that it is not simple to suppress, the KGB campaigns vigorously, employing repression and all other means at its command. The analytical service recommends special measures for this struggle. But even the KGB is powerless finally to suppress nationalism. Where nationalist groups have been discovered and destroyed, new groups arise.

The top secret manual *Fundamentals of Counter-Espionage Activities of KGB Organs* has a bearing on the subject. Under the heading 'The organisation of activity of the counter-espionage apparatus of the KGB against anti-Soviet nationalist elements', it says that the KGB is required to carry out:

1. The struggle against subversive activities of foreign anti-Soviet nationalist centres.

2. The struggle against anti-Soviet nationalist elements on Soviet territory and to employ the necessary prophylaxis.

3. Participation in the ideological destruction of anti-Soviet nationalist elements and the unmasking of their anti-social essence.

Tasks in the struggle against foreign anti-Soviet nationalist centres:

1. To work for the disintegration of foreign nationalist centres.

2. To take steps to stop attempts of foreign organisations to give organisational and ideological support to nationalist elements on Soviet territory.

The struggle against anti-Soviet nationalist elements on Soviet territory includes:

1. Action to stop any attempt by nationalists to create nationalist organisations.

2. The ideological disarmament of nationalists, preparation of material for their public disarmament.

3. Measures designed to split and completely destroy groups and isolate any nationalist activists.

4. To carry out educational and prophylactic work aimed at citizens making any nationalist statements whatsoever.

Measures and tactics aimed at the disintegration of nationalist groups and their ideological disarmament:

1. To introduce via KGB agents, differences and to cause disagreements in nationalist groups.

2. With the help of experienced KGB agents to seize the leadership of nationalist groups.

3. To compromise prominent nationalists in the eyes of their colleagues by their supposed collaboration with KGB organs.

A description of these measures and tactics extends over several more pages of the manual. The aim of all these recommendations is to demonstrate to KGB agents that simple arrest is not sufficient where nationalists are concerned. To be successful in the struggle against a nationalist movement, it has to be destroyed from within without allowing it to organise itself efficiently, by splitting its ranks and by compromising its leaders. Usually they are compromised by means of false documents fabricated by the KGB or with the help of false witnesses who present some recognised authority of the nationalist movement in an unfavourable light. To this end, the KGB employs the dirtiest possible methods, basing its actions on the principle that the end justifies the means.

Life has been particularly unpleasant recently for persons of Jewish nationality. To be a Jew at the present time in the Soviet Union means approximately the same as it meant in Tsarist Russia during the reactionary Stolypin period, 1910-1912, when the very word "Jew" was considered an insult. All manner of restrictions have been introduced: they are not sent to work abroad; not allowed to take part in secret work; forbidden to work on defence projects, and young Jews are frequently denied places in institutes.

Those who apply for exit visas for Israel are regarded by the KGB as enemies. It puts them under round-the-clock observation and collects information in order to be able to put them behind bars. This is done on orders from the Chairman of the KGB. Order No 13 SS of 1973 is entitled *On the Commencement of Operational observation of persons of Jewish nationality who have been refused exit visas to Israel* and is signed: Yu Andropov. If Jews are persecuted by order of the Chairman of the KGB it implies that it is being done with the approval and permission of the Politburo and Soviet Government.

The KGB also gives religious representatives no peace. The Orthodox and Catholic Church, the Lutherans, members of various sects and simple believers of all denominations are all classed as enemies of Communism, and are to be kept under permanent surveillance. How could it be otherwise? They believe in God, a belief categorically denied by Communists. It simply means that they do not fully accept the Communist idea, and do not agree with the teaching of the great Lenin himself. All of this means that they are regarded as a danger, and the avenging sword of the working class, the Cheka, falls upon their heads. But does that avenging sword really belong to the working class?

This is how the KGB functions within a country recognising no law or human rights; employing all its powers and insidious methods; stopping at nothing; rapacious and without mercy. One would have thought that in such an atmosphere no one would dare to embark on anything opposed to the régime.

But in spite of all the KGB's power, in spite of harsh laws and an army of agents and informers, people can be found who speak out against the policies of the Politburo and the Government. There are even those who sometimes attempt to form underground organisations. Yet others, avoiding criticism of the system, simply speak up in defence of the church, of human rights or of some kind of nationalist cause. The majority of such brave souls fall before the avenging arm of the KGB. Many disappear for ever in countless camps or prisons or end their days in psychiatric hospitals or lunatic asylums. They are consumed in today's *Gulag Archipelago*. Few people hear of their fate; the KGB knows how to keep secrets. Those who have managed to save themselves can be counted on one's fingers. These are the people who became known to world opinion like Solzhenitsyn, Maximov, Sakharov and Litvinov. They are the exceptions, while thousands upon thousands of unknown people perish between the KGB millstones. Some day perhaps monuments will be erected in Russia in their honour.

But sometimes the KGB treats even famous people without mercy. Certain facts which at one time were the centre of attention have still never been fully explained, as the truth of the matter was always carefully hidden on the Soviet side and above all by the KGB itself.

There is the case of General Peter Grigorenko who dared to criticise the Soviet leadership, and several times suffered repression and persecution by the KGB. In 1964, on the instructions of the KGB, he was confined for two years in a psychiatric clinic. However, repression and persecution did not break the will of General Grigorenko and after his release from the clinic, he continued his personal war against the Soviet régime. In 1969, he was arrested by the KGB and in February 1970 he was once again declared to be mentally ill and sent for compulsory treatment to a psychiatric clinic in the town of Kazan, in which he was still confined in June 1974. Articles appeared in the Western press about his case. Some wrote that General Grigorenko was a healthy man suffering repression at the hands of the KGB, others cast doubt over his health.

In fact Grigorenko's "mental illness" was invented by the KGB. He became really ill as a result of several years spent in a psychiatric hospital where he was forcibly treated with various medical preparations which destroyed his nervous system. When the former general became only half a man, he was finally freed in the summer of 1974 and Western correspondents were given the opportunity to photograph him so that the world could see his face and its signs of madness. And who would look any better than he did after so many years of maltreatment?

General Grigorenko's case was handled by KGB Colonel Ivan

Tarasovich Shilenko and other officers. Later Shilenko was transferred to the GDR, where from 1968-71 he was Deputy Head of the KGB Special Department for 20th Guards Army and, therefore, at that time one of my chiefs. In 1970, he held an operational seminar for officers of the Special Department located in Bernau, where I was serving. The subject of the conference was "the struggle against anti-Soviet elements among Soviet army troops". The conversation turned to General Grigorenko's case. One of the officers asked Shilenko whether General Grigorenko ever suffered mental disease. Shilenko stated plainly that he *never* had any mental illness, but that he was anti-Soviet and did not agree with Politburo policies. Shilenko explained that it was quite impossible to try an army general for anti-Soviet crimes as that would have attracted the attention of world opinion. For that reason, he was pronounced abnormal and sent for psychiatric treatment where they would "make" him mad. Now Ivan Tarasovich Shilenko has retired on a pension and lives in Moscow.

The case of Pyotr Yakir is another notable example of KGB methods. His father was a famous army commander during the Civil War who in 1937 on Stalin's orders was shot by the Chekists. Ever since his childhood, Yakir himself had wandered from one Soviet prison or forced labour camp to another, starting, it is true, in those designed for children. He had spent the not inconsiderable total of 13 years in such places. After Stalin's death, Yakir was released and his father was rehabilitated. He became an active fighter for justice and for civil rights in the Soviet Union, and for this, he was repeatedly persecuted by the KGB. Nevertheless, he pursued his struggle courageously. In June 1972, it became publicly known that he had once again been arrested and in the summer of 1973 civil proceedings against him were begun. He was charged with working for the Russian anti-Communist organisation, NTS.

The Soviet press published details of the trial of Yakir and of his accomplices. In a speech which was published, Yakir spoke of his mistakes; defended the Soviet social system and made a full admission of his guilt. He was sentenced to three years deprivation of liberty and to three years of exile following his release. Why, after so many years of obstinate struggle, had he suddenly surrendered and accepted his guilt?

The fact was that he had lived through so many trials, prisons, camps, persecutions and many other injustices, that his health had become affected, and there was permanent nervous tension. He could stand it no longer and began to drink too much. The KGB noted the fact and devised a plan. They not only made him an alcoholic, but set an experienced agent to work who turned Yakir into a morphia addict. His will was broken, and he was spiritually destroyed, which explains his behaviour during his trial.

In November 1973, Yakir was released and he is at present living in exile in the Moscow region.

Yakir's case was cited to KGB workers as a good example of how to combat anti-Soviet elements by using all possibilities. All workers involved in the case were highly praised. It was emphasised that not only had they been able to disarm Yakir without creating a commotion, but that they had also compelled him to speak out in public and make a self-accusation.

So in this latter part of the 20th century, the KGB is able to use prisons and camps and send healthy individuals for fearful treatment in psychiatric hospitals and lunatic asylums in defiance of world opinion. It is vital that every possible measure should be taken to stop crimes of this sort; otherwise, what is the point of compiling a "UN Declaration of Human Rights"?

The USSR is indeed a police state, but of a special kind. Firstly, it is well camouflaged on the outside by a thin veneer of democracy. The Constitution is replete with such conceptions as "freedom of the press", "freedom of the individual", "freedom of conscience". All of this was written with world opinion, not the Soviet citizen, in mind. For the citizens, instead of those freedoms "guaranteed" by the Constitution, there is only the KGB, which in practice recognises no laws at all; the militia; the procurator's office; the criminal code and the courts. Adding to the camouflage effect are phrases about brotherhood, freedom, liberty and equality that jump out at you from the vast display of posters all over the Soviet Union.

Secondly, this police state is isolated from the rest of the world. World opinion knows very little of its internal workings. The majority of Soviet citizens live totally isolated from the outside world. From childhood and throughout their lives, they are subjected to intensive propaganda praising the Soviet system as the most just in the world, bringing with it liberation for all mankind; whereas the capitalist world is depicted as being totally inhuman. The ordinary Soviet citizen receives no other trustworthy information about the world. He has no means of getting any; he cannot buy Western newspapers or magazines, and Soviet newspapers usually carry only negative information about the Western world; the unemployed, price rises, crises and so on. This vacuum prevents the man-in-the-street from comparing life in his own country with that in other countries, so he concludes that although his own life is far from easy, and he is frequently deprived of the right to express opinions, he is better off than in the Western world where those "cursed capitalists" do as they please with the workers.

It is true that more recently the flow of information about the outside world has improved a little with the generally improved standards of education and development of communication techniques. A movement for the defence of human rights has arisen amongst the intelligentsia. They demanded more information about world events and democratisation of the Soviet system. The leadership is aware of this and continues energetic opposition to the Western initiative aimed at the free exchange of ideas and information between countries.

Thirdly, the Soviet state is a structure of steps in a pyramid form. At the apex stand the highest Party leaders, the Politburo, Candidate Members of the Politburo and the Government. Party officials of one rank lower status assist them in governing the population. These officials include Secretaries of the CC of the CPSU, secretaries of the Communist Parties of the Union Republics, and, to some extent, the secretaries of the Oblast Committees of the Party and of Krai[1] Committees of the Party who are members of the CC CPSU.

So-called "nomenclature workers" of the CC of the CPSU carry out Party policy in the republics. These workers are Party members who occupy responsible posts falling within the appointment sphere of the CC of the CPSU. Such responsible posts include those of Ministers and Deputy Ministers in the USSR and in the Union Republics, and the majority of responsible posts in industry, the scientific world and the armed forces.

The whole of this Party apparatus, from the Politburo down to the lowest nomenclature worker of the CC CPSU (and of course the majority of KGB workers fall into this category) may be termed a "Mafia" which keeps all the nations of the Soviet Union in subordination and fear. The top ranks of the "Mafia", the Politburo and the Government, enjoy unlimited power. Everything belongs to them, including the people, the country, not to mention their material benefits.

Secretaries of the Communist Parties of the Union Republics and lesser areas do not enjoy the same unlimited power. They have to carry out the will of the top echelons of the "Mafia", but they do command enough power to control the masses over whom they are given sway and they also enjoy enormous material privileges. The other members of the "Mafia" enjoy the rights and privileges which correspond to their position in the hierarchy.

To control the broad mass of the people, they make use of such organs as the police (almost the whole of the KGB belongs to the "Mafia", as it is its bodyguard or avenging arm), the judiciary, the internal troops, the convoy troops and the army. The "Mafia" controls

---

[1] A territorial administrative unit usually containing an autonomous Oblast or region within its boundaries.

the mass information media (radio, press, publishing) which are used in the ideological conditioning of the masses.

The next step down from the "Mafia" is occupied by high-ranking and highly-paid representatives of the heads of large industrial enterprises, a section of top-ranking officers of the armed forces and some scientists, all of whom are Party members. A step lower come the ordinary scientific workers, ordinary officers, engineers and some members of the intelligentsia. And so on down to the very last step, the workers and peasants who also have their own worker aristocracy, activists and shock workers.

Such a step-shaped structure creates its own peculiar system of self-oppression. Representatives of each step in the structure are automatically obliged, because of their fear of losing their privileges, to show their devotion to the system, and to defend it. All this makes it possible for the Politburo and the Soviet Government to keep the masses even more tightly under their control.

Thus, these three additions to the Soviet police system—i.e. its camouflage in the form of a democratic state, its isolation and general deception of the population and the step-shaped structure of society, help to ensure the survival of the system.

CHAPTER 5

At school with the KGB

IN late December 1967, soon after my interview with General Deev, two orders arrived at the unit in which I was serving. One of them was from the Soviet Minister of Defence in which it was stated that I had been discharged from the Soviet Army; and the other was from the Chairman of the KGB, Yury Andropov, confirming my inclusion into the agencies of the Soviet State Security, with retention of my rank as lieutenant.

Within three days, I completed all the formalities in handing over to an officer who had arrived as a replacement. After a farewell party I had arranged in the evening for my friends, my service in the ranks of the Soviet Army came to an end. Next day I reported to the Special Section of the KGB where Lieutenant Colonel Bloshchuk informed me that I was to proceed for training to KGB School No 311 in Novosibirsk, the biggest town in Siberia. It plays a significant role in the economic, political and cultural development of Siberia. In it are to be found largescale heavy industries, the Siberian branch of the Academy of Science of the USSR, scientific research and other institutes. There are also a number of important projects of the defence industry.

Outwardly, the town makes a pleasant impression with wide, straight streets and pale-coloured buildings. During the short summer, with its green parks and alleys, Novosibirsk looks even more attractive. The KGB school, in the main street, named Krasny Prospekt, is in a massive four-storey building standing apart from other houses. Its size is such that it can house all that is necessary for the training and day-to-day life of the KGB students, accommodating the educational block, with its laboratories, class-rooms, lecture and sporting halls, the library, living quarters for officers under training and their mess-hall.

On the day of my arrival at the school, I reported to the duty officer. He checked my papers and recorded me in the list of officers who, at the age of 25, represented a cross-section of the armed forces: motorised-riflemen, missile troops, sailors, frontier guards and many others. Each year the school turns out about 300 KGB officers. Training demanded great effort. We had to master all the techniques of counter-intelligence and the methods of secret police; for, as already mentioned, the KGB is not only concerned with intelligence and counter-intelligence, but it is also the political police. We studied subjects known as "special disciplines". Only some of the studies had overt designations like criminal law, the history of KGB departments, scientific Communism, and criminal proceedings at law. Most of the time was allocated to the study of the special disciplines. Here I want to unveil them:

Special discipline No 1, operational activities of KGB departments.

Special discipline No 2, the intelligence and counter-intelligence departments of the main enemies (USA, German Federal Republic, Britain, France, Israel).

Special discipline No 5, work of the KGB in war.

Special discipline No 6, intelligence activities of the KGB.

And there were many others. Some of these disciplines warrant greater detail.

Special discipline No 1 is the main one in the training of officers at School No 311. Its significance is quite evident from its designation, operational activities of KGB departments. Much attention was paid to counter-intelligence. Here we studied the following questions:

— The task of KGB departments.
— The agents branch of departments (i.e. the selection and preparation of individuals for recruitment as agents, training and education of agents, methods of working with them, etc).
— Conducting various operations (combined operations, "games").
— Misinformation.
— Work against enemy intelligence services.
— Work against anti-Soviet personalities.
— Work against the church and sects.
— Work against the intelligentsia.
— Countering the "ideological diversions" of the enemy.

The KGB makes use of the most varied methods. I want to describe some of those we studied to use in recruiting agents. Two principles govern recruitment: 1, "Idealist-patriotic basis", that is, when the recruitment of an individual is carried out on the basis of his political convictions (Communist, simply a convinced Soviet citizen, friend of and sympathiser with the USSR, this refers to foreigners). 2, "Dependence basis". It is here that the real face of the KGB shows itself. In these cases, it is permissible to resort to everything: blackmail, bribery, and threats, to exert pressure. In this process, great attention is paid to working psychologically; the strong and weak sides of the victim's character are determined, and these are exploited later. For instance, if he is deemed to be a coward, he is intimidated; if he is fond of his relations, then threats are made against them; if he is a careerist, his career is put in jeopardy, and so on.

For blackmail, false documents or photographs manufactured in the KGB laboratories are often used. For the recruitment of men, especially married ones, use is made of women who are instructed to establish intimate relations with the person to be recruited, and the resulting photographs are used for blackmailing him.

However, in recent times, this method often does not achieve the desired results. This is evidently accounted for by the general permissive trend of the last few years, with free love and amorality in matrimonial relations. For instance, a couple of years ago, the KGB made an attempt in this way to recruit one of the foreign diplomats in Moscow, who shall be nameless. A beautiful and clever woman was "prepared" for him. The woman played her part well and said, apparently, that all was going well. The diplomat had been "hooked". He fell under the influence of this woman, and established sexual relations with her. Employees of the KGB's Technical Section managed to take "classic photographs". After all this had been done, the decision was taken that the case had "ripened" and that the diplomat could be recruited.

One day when the diplomat turned up at the flat of his mistress, he was met not by his loved one, but by KGB men. Without wasting words, they went into action. At first an offer was made to the foreign "Romeo" to co-operate on a voluntary basis. On his refusal, he was shown "interesting and unmistakeable photographs" which would compromise him. But this time the trap was sprung in vain: the diplomat said he liked the photographs and would willingly accept several as a souvenir of his conquest, while the KGB could send the rest wherever it liked, to his wife and to his superiors. Learning from such failures, the KGB has lately been making use of this blackmail method less often and with greater caution. To compensate, other brutal methods are being used even more frequently.

The next discipline worth mentioning is "the history of the State Security Departments of the USSR; their work and way of development from the Cheka to the KGB". Those who believe that the history and development of the departments began after the establishment of Soviet power are mistaken. The historical fact that the Cheka (Extraordinary Commission) was established on 20 December 1917 is indisputable.

The structure and tasks of this organisation were quite new. It had to fight for the preservation of the Bolshevik régime. But in *organising its activities,* it made use of many of the methods of the Tsarist *Okhrana* (secret political police). It was not only the Cheka that made use of these methods; they persist to this day, and are being extensively used by the KGB. At the school we had to search the archives of the *Okhrana* (copies, of course). I recollect that we were all astonished at the similarities between the Tsarist system and the KGB's in the way of working with agents. Even the written reports of the *Okhrana* sleuths differed little from the communications of our agents. Moreover, the departments of State Security of the USSR have adopted many other things from the Tsarist experience, so it can be said that the history of the Soviet departments does not begin from the year 1917, but from the times of the *Oprichina* in the reign of Ivan the Terrible. The KGB sticks to many of the old traditions, the cruelty and ruthlessness of the *Oprichina,* the cunning and tricks of the Tsarist *Okhrana,* the implacability and unscrupulousness of Bolshevism towards its enemies.

State Security during these periods was presented to us in a curious way. The activities of the Cheka and Vecheka during the first years of Soviet power in Dzerzhinski's days were studied in detail. Dzerzhinski himself was held up as an ideal Chekist. Many successful operations of his period were described to us.

We got only a superficial account of the activities under Yagoda, Yezhov, Abakumov and Beria (when Stalin was in power); the only comment was that the departments made a number of mistakes during those years. However, it was not the Chekists who were at fault but Stalin, because the NKVD—MGB (People's Commissariat for Internal Affairs—Ministry of State Security, as it was then called) acted in accordance with his orders. Details about these "mistakes" were, naturally, not mentioned to us. To the instructor, Major Aleksandr Sergeevich Larin, they appeared insignificant. It seemed as if as a result of these insignificant "mistakes", only a few persons perished in the camps, and not millions of people. It was in this guileless way that the "glorious" work of the Chekists during Stalinism—involving millions of lives—was portrayed to us. As the Russian proverb says, "When the forest is being cut down, chips fly".[1] The millions of citizens who perished are still called in the USSR "Stalin's chips". In building the new happy socialist society, it was necessary first of all to do away with the capitalist past, and so the human chips flew to prisons, camps, executions.

Only now and then did our instructor, when in a talkative mood, relate some details about those days, and what he had himself gone through and seen. "Yes, those were stormy times. We worked mainly at night. From 10 to 12 in the morning we dealt with papers, till 18 hours, rest. From 18 to 24 hours practical work. Contacts with informers, and each one of us had from 60 to 80 of them, not all of them known by sight as some of them sent us their reports by post. Later, around midnight, the interrogation of those arrested. At the

---

[1] English equivalent is "You cannot make an omelette without breaking eggs."

end of such a working day, we reported to our superiors how many reports we had collected during the day, how many confessions had been obtained from those arrested. The more such results the employee produced, the more valuable he was considerd to be."

In reply to our question whether it was permitted to beat and torture arrested persons, he replied simply: "Yes, this was an obligatory and daily phenomenon." When asked whether he himself had resorted to such methods, Major Larin, as was to be expected, replied: "Personally, I did not beat anyone, I managed without it." None of us believed him and talked about this openly. Many thought that Larin himself had been under arrest. Lately, there has been a good deal of talk in the KGB on this subject, not in a critical sense, but rather with a nuance of regret that now such measures could not be used openly.

The KGB, as one of the most important branches of the state essential to the régime, selects its men with great thoroughness. Intelligence, counter-intelligence and political control of the population demand highly qualified specialists loyal to the existing system. The KGB leadership appreciates this fully and does not stint manpower or resources for training. The future employee must have a good general education; be intelligent and possess such qualities as self-reliance, self-control, a capacity for establishing connections, resolution and courage. The main aspect is the political reliability of the candidate. All these requirements present the personnel department with a problem of enormous complexity. In the Soviet Union there are more than enough people with good general education, intelligence and intiative, but only a small percentage are convinced Communists. On the other hand, among the convinced Communists absolutely loyal to the régime, there are often individuals whose personal qualifications do not meet the essential requirements.

Preference is given to the convinced Communists, following the principle that it is better to have fewer successes, making up for this by having a reliable, tested organisation. However, the KGB would not have been able to function so successfully without the help of the second group, namely those who have become Communists out of necessity. They reason that "as one is living in a Communist state and wants to attain something in life, you have to be a Communist". This does not mean that they are enemies of Communism or of the régime; I would describe them as opportunist or "pro forma Communists", who show little concern for political problems; paying more attention to their own personal affairs, including professional success.

I would estimate the percentage proportion of representatives of the two groups among KGB employees as 70: 30 in favour of the so-called "convinced Communists". I say "so-called" because their conviction is often based on what can be gained; they have definite privileges and are, therefore, satisfied with Communism. Of really convinced Communists, very few remain; the days of Pavel Korchagin have passed into history.

I have shown the most striking differences, but in life the demarcation line is often difficult to find. The question "who is really who" in most cases remains unanswered. It is especially difficult to get an answer to this question under the conditions prevailing in a dictatorship, where most people take great care to conceal their real political convictions.

The "convinced Communist" group is, as a rule, satisfied with the status quo, its position, privileges, and power over others. They work hard and all of them (with very few exceptions) serve their time safely to pensionable age. The exceptions are those who take advantage of their service status, appropriate public money or resort to extortion. They are liable to be discharged prematurely. If they do not have influential relations, they do not achieve a great career; the "ceiling" for them is the rank of colonel.

The "unconvinced Communists" find themselves in a different situation. After three to five years' service, many come to realise that the KGB is concerned not only with intelligence and counter-intelligence, but with the ruthless suppression of the slightest attempt by citizens to show any kind of opposition to the injustices of the régime. Sooner or later they are faced with the question: "What to do?" By that time, some of them have been corrupted by the sense of power over others and eventually work diligently, often achieving a good career in this way. Others have families and consequently, despite being conscious of the injustices, continue to carry out their duties.

But a small percentage in this group cannot live with their consciences and resort to radical measures. Some become alcoholics; others contrive to get their discharge, and some not only sever their connection with the KGB but with the whole system and go over to the West.

The group in which I found myself under training at School No 311 comprised 26 persons. What was their fate after five years of practical work? I cannot say what happened to all of them, but what I know about some of them is enough to confirm my conclusions. One of them, Vladimir Kornilin, managed to get himself discharged on the grounds that he did not have the qualities of a counter-intelligence officer. The second, Vladimir Maksimovich Bykov, after becoming disillusioned with his work which he latterly did not hide, began to drink heavily; stopped working and was discharged. A third member of that group myself—turned up in the West.

Representatives of the most varied sections of Soviet society find themselves working for the KGB. They include children of workers and peasants (very rarely), of the intelligentsia, and, more often, sons of party and other important functionaries. All of them must, of course, to some extent have the qualities demanded of them. A person whose parents have lived abroad; have been tried in court or who are specially recorded by the KGB in the lists of suspects, cannot become an employee. The question of nationality also plays a big part. For instance, the doors are closed to Crimean Tartars and Jews, giving a hollow ring to the slogan "Brotherhood, Equality, Happiness of all the peoples".

Employees of secret services are often described in stories of adventure, and in films, as "supermen" who are always shooting, chasing after someone or escaping from pursuit. I will not disillusion readers by asserting that this is not so, for there are such occasions, but very seldom. The first priority is intellectual work, demanding great patience. The winner is the one who methodically overcomes his enemy, by anticipating his intentions. The work of intelligence and counter-intelligence is, first of all, a battle of wits. Operatives are called upon to show an ability to analyse and evaluate events or facts, to think in reverse, to draw correct and timely conclusions. The main implements are often paper and pencil. They tried to teach us all this at school, and it must be said that our instructors were successful. The majority of them were officers with great practical experience in counter-intelligence work and sound theoretical grounding. Almost all were good methodologists.

Our schooling consisted of lectures, seminars and training in practical operations. The seminars were particularly interesting, always lasting several hours. Each trainee had to solve an operational problem alone and to expound his solution in the form of a concept on paper. Then the instructor would call upon several trainees to explain their solutions. After this, a free discussion started. Each expressed his own opinion, and was himself subjected to criticism. This method compelled each trainee to take an active part throughout the whole of his schooling. We developed the quality of independence, ability to find the best solution to a problem, to appraise our actions and the possible actions of the enemy.

In learning ways of recruiting agents, great attention was paid to the psychological aspect of how to arrive at a correct appreciation and description of the potential recruit, and the ability to fathom his real self and his views on life. Training in this sense was carried out not only theoretically but in practice. For instance, we were asked to select a "target" for recruitment from among the cadets, and then to indicate the most promising method. In this way, instructors not only inculcated methods of recruitment, but gained an insight into the characters of future officers with the help of their own colleagues.

The person in charge of the secret library of the school at the time was a woman, a spinster of about 40. Because her private life had been unfortunate, her attitude towards men was sceptical. For several years, the instructors used her in the role of a candidate for recruitment. One of the pupils would "recruit" her in a room equipped with a television camera and microphones. The others remained in the lecture room and watched the "recruitment" on the television screen. For those sitting in the room this was an entertainment, but not for the pupil. Having been "recruited" hundreds of times, the library woman knew her role very well, while the trainee knowing that his actions were being watched by his comrades often stammered or forgot his lines. It then depended on the woman; often her conduct and replies not only compelled the trainee to abandon the "recruitment", but proved to him that it was unnecessary. Such an outcome caused the spectators much amusement and the unlucky wretch had to bear much teasing later.

We had arrived at Novosibirsk from various parts of the Soviet Union; from the western frontier of the USSR and from the Far East, from the southern part of the country and the North. About 80 per cent of us were married, but as we were not permitted to bring wives with us, there was little difference between single and married officers. We all lived in officers' quarters, two or three to a room. Conditions were the same for all, and on Sundays men went off to the town for "free hunting", the current term applied to making the acquaintance of a woman. This did not commit us to anything and was terminated after a couple of months of so. To avoid any complications, the governing body advised trainees to steer clear of permanent attachments.

Although throughout the training period we remained together for a whole year, no special friendships were formed; everyone lived for himself, putting little trust in the others. This was understandable for among the trainees were many voluntary "informers". Conversations were usually trivial. Friendship had to be between two, so that in the event of a denunciation it became clear at once who was responsible.

The evenings were usually spent playing cards. The exceptions were the first few evenings after pay-day which were a bright interlude in the gloomy barrack life of young officers. From early morning, vodka was bought and in the evening a general drinking bout started. The governing body was, of course, aware of this, but no one took steps against the practice. And this was a correct decision: our instructors chose the lesser of two evils. If the trainees had been forbidden to consume spirits at the school, then most of them would have started to drink inordinately in the town. Yet despite such subterfuges by the governing body, it nevertheless had enough troubles with the trainees.

After three to four months training at the school, many of us understood that we belonged to an élite with great rights. Although we still did not have identity cards as KGB men, this did not stop some trainees from trying to test the power of the three magic letters. Once, after a payday, one of the trainees, Vladimir Vorontsov, after drinking spirits, turned up in a "happy" state at one of the town's cafes and demanded that several tables should be freed immediately for a specially important KGB operation. The manager naturally wanted the doubtful Chekist to produce an identity card. Instead, he got a blow in the face and a fight started. Soon the police arrived and the trainee was taken back to the school. Next day he was severely reprimanded and the incident was then forgotten. This was the usual procedure for such incidents.

I established fairly close relations with Vladimir Bykov, who was in my group. We spent many evenings together. He was trusting and often expressed his opinion on various questions. He read a great deal. At that time he was enchanted with the KGB, often mentioning this to me. Though I did not feel that way, I never attempted to argue about this for obvious reasons. In the end Bykov's views changed radically as I was able to observe for myself because we landed in the same section—but more of that later.

Our training was coming to an end. Passing out examinations were impending, and after that postings. In spite of the doubts in a corner of my mind about the Soviet régime, the training at the school and the mastering of the art of counter-intelligence aroused an interest in me. So I studied successfully; passed out as one of the best trainees at the end of 1968, and awaited posting to one of the sections of the Third Directorate. We had at the outset of our training been told that we would go back to work in the sections from which we had been sent to the school, but now rumours spread that about 20 men would have to serve at strategic missile bases. None of us wanted to be selected for these bases because, usually, they are far from inhabited places and officers are obliged to live for a long time away from the civilised world. Each one of us thought: "As long as it's not me."

At last, posting day arrived. We were assembled in one of the schools halls and the names were read out. I awaited the decision about my fate with impatience, but to my alarm my name was not called. "Can it really be to missile troops?" I wondered. Just then the school's commandant, Colonel Voronov, announced that those officers whose names had not been mentioned must report to him. It turned out that there were five of us, including Bykov. The commandant informed us that we, as the best trainees, were to be posted abroad. "Where you are actually going, you will find out in Moscow, in the central organisation of the KGB." But first we were given a month's leave.

I spent my leave in Moscow and at the end of January went off to the Personnel Directorate of the KGB. The central organisation is in a massive building in Dzerzhinski Square. To gain admission a single certificate is not enough; it is also necessary to have a special pass, issued in the passes bureau of the KGB. After completing all the formalities, I received a pass on which was recorded my surname, the number of the entrance to the building, the floor and number of the room in which I was expected.

On each floor, my papers were carefully checked by sentries. It seemed that these checks would never end. But eventually I found my way to a room where I was received by a lieutenant-colonel. He asked me to sit down; checked my papers and put them in one of the drawers in his desk. Noticing my look of surprise, he said that they would no longer be needed by me, as I would be issued with new ones.

He expressed interest in the way I had spent my leave, and inquired about my health. I answered that everything had gone normally for me, while I thought to myself: "Why does he spin out time, instead of starting straight away to talk business." As if reading my thoughts, the colonel told me that I was being posted to work in the German Democratic Republic. The necessary documents were already completed and he handed them to me. I was ordered to arrive on 2 February 1969 in Potsdam and to report to the Directorate of Special Sections of the KGB of the Group of Soviet Forces in Germany. I got no further instructions. The colonel said that I would be given all details in Potsdam. The same evening I left on the Moscow-Wunsdorf train for Potsdam.

CHAPTER 6

Recruitment by conviction or force

ON 2 February 1969, at about 06.00 hours, the train drew in at the station of the small village called Wunsdorf, where, since the war years, the headquarters of the Group of Soviet Forces in Germany (GSFG) have been situated. A car sent by the KGB Directorate was already waiting for me at the station, and was easily located by its number, given to me in Moscow.

In the car was an officer who checked my documents. Then we set off and in about an hour arrived in Potsdam. The KGB Directorate attached to the GSFG was near the town centre. It occupied a considerable area and was bounded by a high fence. I was received by the duty officer, who found me a room in a hotel and said that I was required to report that day at 09.00 hours to the head of the Directorate, Major-General Titov.

A pleasant surprise awaited me at the hotel. Bykov was there; that very same Bykov who studied with me in the school. It emerged that, like me, he had been assigned to work in the GDR and had arrived the day before. We were delighted to see each other again. I asked him whether he had been given a definite appointment in a Department, but he said "Not yet", and that everything was to be decided today. He was also to report to the general at nine o'clock. We determined to get assigned to the same Department.

At nine o'clock, we arrived at the general's office, cleanly shaven, in carefully ironed uniforms and with our hair neatly combed. The duty officer informed us that the general expected us. The general invited us to sit down at a table and inquired about our health. Generally speaking, it was the same old conventional beginning to a conversation. He briefly reminded us of the responsible nature of our work, particularly abroad, then wished us every success and the conversation was ended. As we were later to understand, the brief encounter with the general had an educational purpose: it was meant to show young officers what consideration was shown to them as well as what a responsible position they held.

We received from Colonel Kostin, head of the Cadre Department of the KGB Directorate, all necessary details and were given our appointments. The colonel was short, fat and completely bald. His eyes were of indeterminate colour and had no flicker of life. He created the impression of being a typical apparatchik, used to living according to instructions from above, avoiding any personal initiative. This later proved to be a true impression. In about 20 minutes, the question of our appointment was decided: we were both to work in the department handling the 6th Motorised Rifle Guards Division. The Department was located at Bernau. A car from there was to collect us at 13.00 hours.

Colonel Kostin, as a cadre officer, then switched the conversation to indoctrination. For the next two hours, Bykov and I had to listen to loud praises of the Politburo, the KGB leadership and the government. There was also high praise for Chekists' honourable work. During this time Kostin, without apparently noticing, repeated the same thing about three times. Finally, when Bykov and I had lost all hope of ever leaving his office, the talk ended. When we got out we looked at each other, our eyes bemused by such a chat and then burst out laughing. "Some talk that," I remarked. "The old man's probably gone a bit off his head," was Bykov's comment.

Nothing remained in our heads of all those loud-sounding but empty phrases which Kostin poured over us for two hours. Any speech made up of such commonplace expressions, devoid of real meaning, is always difficult to remember, especially if it is in turgid Party language, with words like Party, Communism, Socialism, Congress, Politburo repeated a hundred times.

When we returned to our hotel, an officer from Bernau who had come to collect us was waiting. He was about 40, tall and kindhearted looking. "Captain Davydov," he said introducing himself. "Ah, so you are coming to work in our department? That's good. Tell me, did you bring some of our Russian vodka with you?"

When we replied in the affirmative, he promptly suggested that then and there we should drink to our meeting. I took a bottle of vodka from my case and poured some into glasses standing on the table. I naturally gave more to Davydov than to ourselves and without unnecessary words, we drained them dry. Ten minutes later we climbed into the Gazik which had been waiting for us. Davydov ordered the driver "Home to Bernau" and at about 14.00 hours we left Potsdam. "At 17.00 hours, we shall be there," Davydov announced.

Bernau is about 20 kilometres to the north-east of Berlin, making it about 100 km from Potsdam. There were two ways of getting there, either via Berlin or by-passing Berlin. Davydov announced that he wished to show us Berlin, so we chose the first route. Our Gazik sped merrily along the motorway. After the vodka he had drunk Davydov was in a happy mood, talking away and even singing. After an hour's drive, I asked Davydov when we would finally reach Berlin. "What time is it?" he asked me. "It's already three o'clock,"

I replied.

"Three! " exclaimed Davydov. With that, he told the driver to stop the car; took out a map and, after some thought, announced that we had "slightly" lost our way. Instead of driving towards Berlin, we had been driving in the opposite direction towards Leipzig for a whole hour. Davydov cursed the driver and having turned the car round, we drove off in the right direction. Then we found that neither Davydov nor the driver knew the way in Berlin. To add to our confusion, it became dark. Davydov stopped the car near an old woman and we awaited Davydov's conversation in German. We waited in vain. Although he had been two years in Germany, the only word pronounced by Davydov in German was "Frau". Verbatim his question was as follows: "Frau, how to go [in Russian] to Bernau?" The old woman started to say something quickly in German. Davydov kept nodding and repeating in Russian "Yes, yes, yes! " Then he slammed the car door and told the driver to drive on. "Where?" "How do I know?" In fact, he did not understand a word of German, but he did not seem offended by our laughter, only muttering that it was high time the East Germans learned to speak Russian. For about two hours, we drove around aimlessly until a signpost pointing to Bernau saved us. At about 21.00 hours, we arrived at the Special Department for the 6th Motorised Rifle Division, housed in a small two-storey detached villa, standing in a garden surrounded by a high fence.

Both Bykov and I felt tired from the journey and, therefore, went to bed immediately, looking forward to a peaceful night. However, our hopes proved to be premature. At about two o'clock, we were awakened by a loud knock and a senior lieutenant stood before us. "Get up you devils," he shouted. "Let's get acquainted."

It was obvious that he was rather tipsy. His overcoat was unbuttoned, his cap was askew and his face was smiling in welcome. "Koroteyev is my name," he stammered, "Kostya" (short for Konstantin). He offered me an opened bottle of cognac. There were no glasses to hand and I had two mouthfuls straight from the bottle. It was cheap GDR cognac, the taste was awful. Noticing my grimace, Kostya said: "Never mind chaps, you'll get used to it," then he embraced us and disappeared.

"What a man," said Bykov. "He is so drunk that he stammers."

However, it later emerged that Kostya had stammered since childhood.

Next day, we were summoned by Major Aleksandr Petrovich Boychenko, head of the KGB Department. I had to go in first. Boychenko was tall, well-built and dark-skinned. There was something Asiatic about his features although by nationality he was Ukrainian.

I liked his eyes, which were attentive and clever. During our conversation, he was always in motion, indicating an energetic personality.

He listened carefully as I said my piece, and he made notes. He asked in detail about my studies at the school. He told me that I was assigned to three battalions of the 82nd Motorised Rifle Guards Regiment, quartered in Bernau itself. Davydov looked after the Regimental Headquarters and its remaining detachments. In future, I had to co-ordinate my work closely with him. This pleased me as I liked Davydov. Boychenko asked whether, as a KGB officer, I knew what were my particular tasks.

I replied: "Of course I do. We were taught that at the school." "Good," said Boychenko. "All you studied at the school was high theory, here in contrast practical work begins and that, brother, is altogether another matter." He asked me to pay particular attention while he outlined my tasks and the peculiarities of Special Department work in the GDR.

"Your tasks include: first, to prevent, in the battalions assigned to you, Western espionage agencies from recruiting any Soviet citizen whatsoever, be it military or civilian. Second, if it so happens that Western agencies have already recruited someone then it is your business to find that person and render him harmless. Third, seek out anti-Soviets, the enemies of Soviet power. Fourth, seek out Western espionage agency agents among East German nationals residing near your charges. And what do you need to solve all these problems?" he asked.

"A good agent network supplying me with the necessary information and . . ." Boychenko interrupted with: "Quite right. You need agents, more agents and yet more agents."

He explained that the units assigned to me previously had no officer in charge of them because of the shortage of KGB staff, and that in them there was not a single agent either among the Soviet citizens or among the surrounding German nationals. Such a state of affairs meant many difficulties for me; without secret sources of information, I would have to seek out suitable candidates and recruit them. This was not easy. Meanwhile, Boychenko continued to announce new "joys" to me.

"You must commence active work and create a good agent apparatus in the shortest possible time. You must recruit ten agents in two months." "In two months?" I asked him, reflecting that this was an impossible task, for it normally takes three or four months to recruit *one* agent. Of course, four or five people can be simultaneously prepared for recruitment and then they can be recruited in five or six months. But to get ten agents in two months, that would be breaking all the rules. I told Bolchenko so. But my words had no effect. "Yes, that's right, ten agents and you must do it in two months. In that time you must recruit three officers, two regular service men, one private, two officers' wives and two German nationals."

My further objections were cut short with the question: "Do you know what the three letters KGB mean?" "Yes sir," I replied. "The State Security Committee."

"No! KGB means Office of Crude Bandits" (*Kontora Grubykh Banditov*). After a couple of years work, every KGB worker knows that. We must work with impertinence, putting the pressure on, fully conscious of our power. When recruiting agents, you must not only convince them but also compel them to work for us. KGB has enough power for that. If you work on that principle you will successfully fulfil the task I have placed before you."

For the next half-hour, he continued to explain that the recruitment of Soviet citizens, particularly servicemen, was not a complicated affair; almost every citizen, even if he did not wish to co-operate, could be compelled to do so. The KGB had the rights and the power needed. If it was an officer, then his career could be threatened (without KGB approval no officer can be sent to a military academy or get promotion). With regular servicemen, it was even simpler; they could just be dismissed from the army. Any Soviet citizen's life, too, could be threatened; he could be barred from an institute or from work in any undertaking, or be forbidden to travel abroad.

"Therefore," Boychenko maintained, "if you use your rights and your power skilfully, you will recruit ten agents in two months." He went into detail on how I must behave. "Don't forget you are a KGB officer. Everything at your place of work, beginning with the unit commander and ending with the last dirty private, depends in one way or another on you. You are a free agent. Therefore, behave in a confident manner and if needs be with impertinence and crudeness. You are a defender of the Soviet régime. You have the power to determine the political reliability of others and, therefore, frequently their fate as well. So now get to work, Comrade Lieutenant. Providing you defend it, the Soviet régime permits you to do almost everything."

"In spite of the fact that the GDR is officially an independent state we, the KGB, have many rights here and can work almost as if we were back home in the USSR." Boychenko took from his safe a document based on the secret agreement between the Soviet Union and the GDR. In effect the KGB:

— Has the right to operate among German nationals in order to unmask the agents of Western espionage services or persons of anti-Soviet or anti-socialist tendencies.

— Has the right to recruit GDR nationals to be used in espionage

activities directed against Western countries (Federal German Republic, USA, Britain, France, etc).
— Can recruit visitors from capitalist countries on GDR soil.
— Is allowed to have "conspiratorial" flats.
— Can actively co-operate with the GDR KGR (MfS) and is permitted to consult MfS card indexes. On request, MfS opens the correspondence and monitors telegraphic communications of GDR citizens where these are of interest to the KGB.
— Is permitted to consult GDR police records and enjoys its active police support. MfS has no rights whatsoever insofar as the KGB is concerned. They can only ask.

At the end of the document, KGB officers were recommended to behave politely and respectfully towards MfS officials, a cynical gesture after all that had been said in the document.

Speaking of Germans as agents, Boychenko said: "A German is just like a Russian; he also wants to live and does not want unpleasantness." Once again, the same methods as with our own citizens; if not by conviction then by force. He went on: "Sometimes it is easier to recruit Germans than Russians. They are a disciplined people and respect strength; so, when recruiting them, behave confidently, show them our strength. It helps."

When I told him I did not speak German, Boychenko said 80 per cent of the Department's officers did not speak the language, although they all worked with Germans. The problem was solved by having an officer translator attached to each operational worker. "And in one year, you are obliged to speak German, then that difficulty disappears."

He added that, at first, he would meet me almost daily. Then he sent me to see his deputy, Major Kryukov, who was a couple of years older than Boychenko. Outwardly he looked intelligent, although his face spoke eloquently of his love for drink. His movements showed that he was an experienced *apparatchik*. "Aleksandr Gerasimovich," he said introducing himself. "Please sit down." I learned that I had been given two days to settle my affairs, and that a flat was ready for me. He told me that there were 17 people working in the Department, and that basically relations between them all were good. He sent me to the Department's secretary who, against my signature, handed me the key of the safe and some documents.

At last I found myself among my future colleagues. About five of them were gathered in one of the Department's rooms. One of them was Koroteyev, sober this time. I had to answer many questions as most of them had not been in the USSR for about a year. I particularly liked senior Lieutenant Lavrukhin who stood out from the others by his tidy appearance and wit. Koroteyev hinted that to get better acquainted I should invite everyone over some evening for a glass of vodka. It was decided that we would meet at my place the day after tomorrow.

In a short while, Bykov appeared. He had been appointed to a unit which was located about 40 kilometres from Bernau. Later Davydov and I set off for my new flat. He asked about my conversation with Boychenko. When I told him about the ten agents I had to recruit in two months, he laughed. "That's how to teach you young chaps to work, the head knows what he is doing." But he added that I should not worry as Boychenko set high targets on purpose so as to make his officers work harder. "If, during that time, you recruit five agents, then the head will be pleased."

That evening Davydov and I sat in my new flat. A half-empty bottle of vodka stood on the table in front of us and quiet music came from the radio. The atmosphere was cosy and encouraged conversation. Davydov was lounging in an armchair with a smoking cigar in his hand. I noted that alcohol put him in good mood, and after the third glass he asked that we use the familiar "thou" instead of the more formal "you" in Russian. He said I should call him Lev, and went on to describe the setup in the Department. "It is double-headed," he explained, "and there is continual war between the head, Boychenko, and his deputy Kryukov." From what he said, it was obvious that Major Boychenko, energetic and fairly young, was out to make a successful career in the KGB. For this, the first requirement was that his Department should produce successes. These could be achieved only if his officers diligently sought out "enemies" of the state, for successes are measured by the number of enemy elements, agents of Western agencies or so-called anti-Soviet elements, who are discovered and unmasked. So he spared no effort, with orders, pep-talks, rewards and punishments, and personal example. He worked night and day and demanded the same of his officers. Boychenko had help in other ways: his wife's brother held a post in the Supreme Soviet, and good connections play a decisive role under Soviet conditions in obtaining a "warm" place. So Boychenko could see himself in future with colonel's or even general's epaulettes.

According to Davydov, Kryukov was also a "hard nut". He worked at one time in the Moscow KGB headquarters, but committed errors and was down-graded, although he kept the rank of major, and was sent to work in the GDR. Although he had suffered a misfortune, he nevertheless had many KGB friends in Moscow who did not forget him. Kryukov had been, to some extent, "spoiled" by having been at the top, and could not resign himself to his present post. He refused to recognise Boychenko as his chief. He did not particularly want to work; he was just waiting for his pension, and in the meantime drank. Conflicts often arose between the two men and their quarrels were sometimes heated.

In Davydov's view, the other officers exploited this situation. When it came to solving problems, what the head would not authorise his deputy approved two or three days later, and vice versa. Sometimes this game played by their subordinates passed off smoothly without being noticed, but sometimes it was noticed by the offended side, which promptly led to a row between the two bosses.

"However strange it may seem," said Davydov, "sometimes they both forget their enmity for a while and together they go off somewhere on a drinking spree. The soak lasts several days. At such times, we don't work either."

Davydov spoke well of Lavrukhin, saying he was a good chap who not only knew how to work, but knew how to show off his work. "Work alone does not mean anything if you don't know how to show it off. You need to know the art of showing off your work, of showing your brilliant results to impress your chiefs: that is the most important thing for a successful career."

He described one officer of the Department, senior Lieutenant Zemskov, as the chief's favourite who, on occasion, informed on his comrades. "Be careful with him, he's a cunning fellow."

"And what is Koroteyev like?" I asked. "Koroteyev, he's a real find for the Department." And then Davydov told me his story. Koroteyev was the son of a colonel-general who had died about ten years before. In his day, Koroteyev senior had been a great friend of the present head of the KGB Directorate, Major-General Titov. For this reason, Kostya was under his wing and made every use of the fact. He hardly worked at all, was permanently drunk yet was never reprimanded. Boychenko did not know what to do with him.

Davydov's assessments were fairly objective. The only false piece of information was about Zemskov, who turned out to be a splendid fellow and never informed on anybody, whereas Davydov himself did, not because he wished to achieve something for himself, but simply because it was a sort of illness which he had, as I learned later.

The two free days I had been given passed quickly. As agreed, on one of the evenings all the officers I had invited, came to my flat. There were eight of them. The fact is that only ten people actually worked in Bernau; the remainder worked on the periphery such as in Frankfurt, Eberwalde and Berlin and contact between the groups was only on a business level. This was why the ten in Bernau formed the collective's nucleus and they regularly spent their free time together. So they came to my place. The evening passed in friendly fashion. I met Lieutenant Nalishkin, the Department's translator, who was short, strong, very calm and talked little. He agreed to help me study German. Zemskov, tall with red hair, was also there and was obviously respected. It may be said that I found the evening useful; it helped me to join in with the collective.

Next day my KGB work started.

CHAPTER 7

Traps for the unwary

BEFORE getting down to the task of setting up a viable agent network, I had to master the situation in the unit and its environment. I began by seeking data about the personnel and the characteristics of local German citizens. I had to study the "Classified file" for the unit. This was several tomes of secret documents of between 2,000 to 3,000 pages, covering information vital for determining the concrete objectives of the KGB.

Operational intelligence about the personnel, which was absolutely vital to me in preparing recruitments, revealed the total numbers of officers, soldiers and employees working in the unit and also their qualitative composition. Special attention was paid to the "nationalities" question. I have already indicated what an important role this plays in the lives of Soviet citizens. Not all nationalities enjoy the confidence of the authorities; preference is given to Russians, Ukrainians and White Rusisans (excluding the Western Ukraine and Western White Russia). Jews, Crimean Tartars, Latvians, Lithuanians, Estonians and those with their origins in the regions of the Western Ukraine and Western White Russia are suspect; anyone serving in the army who falls into such categories receives special attention from the KGB. It strives to place reliable agents among them to restrict their service advancement.

For example, an obscure government directive forbids the posting abroad of officers and soldiers of Jewish nationality. It is also forbidden to assign Soviet citizens of German nationality to serve with troops stationed in the GDR. All this is taken into account in the analysis of personnel and the data, together with recommendations, is then concentrated in the "Classified file". The number of Jews, Latvians, Crimean Tartars serving in the unit is shown there: so is the number of agents required to report on them.

The file also contains a list of those who, in the opinion of the KGB, are potentially unreliable: those who have at any time expressed the least displeasure with authority, or who have been tried for any sort of offence, and those with relatives who are living or have lived abroad. People maintaining any sort of contact with East Germans, and still more so with citizens of capitalist countries, are listed in it.

My unit's brief on the German population living in the vicinity identified individuals who had relatives in West Germany or any other capitalist country; those previously convicted of crimes; individuals who had ever travelled abroad to a capitalist country and also GDR citizens who had any contact with Soviet military personnel. It also identified German shops and public houses patronised by Soviet citizens, and listed German women of easy virtue who regularly consorted with Soviet officers and soldiers, and more serious data vital to the organisation of counter-espionage. Special interest was taken in enemy intelligence activities against a military unit; in recruitment attempts by NATO intelligence among Soviet military personnel; and in individuals, both German and Soviet citizens, suspected of working for Western intelligence services.

After an exhaustive study of the file, I set about acquainting myself with the men of the unit. I began with Colonel Nikishkin, commanding officer of the 83rd Motorised Rifle Regiment, and experienced for the first time what power is locked into those simple words KGB, even for me, a raw lieutenant of 24 whose mother's milk, as the saying goes in Russia, had scarcely dried on my lips, meeting a grey-haired colonel. Before describing our talk, it must be pointed out that officers of the Third Directorate of the KGB serving with Soviet troops each wear, for purposes of disguise, normal military uniform in no way distinguishable from that of other army officers.

So, when I appeared unexpectedly in Colonel Nikishkin's office, he stared at me angrily and barked: "What do you want, Comrade Lieutenant, can't you see I am busy? Report to me later." When I said that I was an officer of the KGB and was to work with his regiment in the coming year, the expression on Nikishkin's face was at once transformed; it became friendly and somehow obsequious. "Please come in, Comrade Lieutenant, for you I have always got time. I am very glad to make your acquaintance," he fawned on me. He began to take an interest in whether I was getting myself properly organised in my new post, inquiring if my quarters were well-equipped and if there was anything at all that I needed. He expressed a readiness to assist me in any possible way he could.

The insincere turn which the conversation had taken had an unpleasant effect on me; I felt ashamed of the colonel and his fear of me and tried to bring the conversation with him to an end as quickly as possible. But I was only just at the beginning of exchanges like these. Other officers behaved in precisely the same way. To begin with, this produced an unpleasant impression although, to be frank, it also gave one a pleasant consciousness of one's own authority and power. After working for approximately 18 months in the KGB, I accepted all this as being quite commonplace and my rightful due.

I soon got quite a good picture of the situation in the unit and gradually got down to preparations for recruitments among the officers, soldiers and employees. It took me two weeks to select several officers and soldiers whom I could begin to make ready, and in under a month—an unusually short period—they had been recruited and had begun active collaboration with the KGB. Direct recruitment of military personnel is not a complicated business. To begin with, the greatest difficulty lies in the correct choice of informant. He must possess those qualities which are vital for an agent, but he must also be in touch with those who are of special interest to the KGB. In recruitments, great care is devoted to conspiracy. The value of an agent lies in his being "unblown" as an informant to those around him, yet he must enjoy the confidence of those in whom the Department is interested. Colonel Boychenko was following my activities throughout this time with special care and was pleased with the results. My recruitment of agents depended not only on my ability as a counter-intelligence officer, but on the authority and power of the KGB. In practice one rarely comes across a Soviet citizen who refuses to co-operate with the notorious Chekists. Everyone thinks about the consequences and of his own future.

Faced with the necessity of having a good agent in the headquarters of the 16th Motorised Rifle Regiment who would furnish me with vital information about its officers, my choice fell on the chief of the motor transport wing, Major Mezentsev. I was decisively influenced by his lively and sociable personality: he had many friends among the officers at regimental headquarters and he enjoyed their confidence, but at the same time he had contrived to achieve good relations with the higher command. Success on both these contrasting fronts demands a special sort of resourcefulness and, I would say, almost actor-like qualities. Mezentsev possessed all of these. He was always in the know about events and intrigues that occurred in the life of the regiment. Many officers turned to him for advice. He tried to satisfy them all, but not because he genuinely wanted to assist someone. He was no idealist; he would dish out help only to put others in his debt. His motto was: "Today I will help you, but don't you forget that tomorrow you are obliged to help me."

In a nutshell, his qualities suited him perfectly for work as an agent. I began gradually to prepare his recruitment. Inconspicuously, I assembled from various sources a full personality description. I studied carefully his service record which I obtained on a plausible pretext from the personnel section in headquarters. From this study, I hit upon two areas of compromising material which could be exploited in his recruitment. The first was his friendship with one of the GDR citizens, through whom he was organising the sale of gold rings, coffee and radio receivers to Germans. The other was the fact that his brother had been sentenced several years previously to two years in a labour camp for robbery. Mezentsev had taken great care to hide this information, which I gleaned from a special card index, fearing that it could damage his career.

I found no other black marks in his biography. But these would more than suffice to wreck his service career should this prove necessary. I met him on several occasions under various plausible pretexts such as games of billiards and chess, and chatted to him on innocuous subjects. At these meetings, Mezentsev was reserved and I had the feeling that he was frightened of the KGB, so I decided to exploit this factor. Soon, everything was ready for his recruitment in the officers' mess where I made use of the office of the chief of the officers' mess, who was on leave. One evening, Mezentsev was there as usual and I found him playing billiards. I chose a moment when he was on his own and asked him if he could spare a few minutes. He, of course, agreed—rarely does an officer refuse to collaborate—and we marched into the chief's office.

I closed the door behind me: "So that no one else can disturb us," I explained to Mezentsev when I noticed his startled expression. Knowing that he was frightened, I decided to recruit him without any "diplomatic" ruses. Having chatted for a while on general subjects, I explained to him briefly and simply that I wanted him to co-operate with the KGB. To begin with, he tried to prevaricate, saying that he was extremely busy and that his health was bad. I retaliated by declaring that if he did not wish to collaborate, I had sufficient means at my disposal to force him to do so. It only required one such threatening sentence to break his resistance. "Good, then I will work for the KGB," he sighed, "only I am afraid that someone else will get to hear of it." "No one else will know," I reassured him. "Just put your signature here, that you wish to co-operate voluntarily." He did so without a further word. His attitude infuriated me; I was expecting a struggle, but instead got a cowardly, servile readiness to co-operate. Subsequently, he collaborated under the pseudonym Krasnopolsky. His fear of the KGB never left him.

Of course, not everyone recruited behaves like that. Sometimes one comes across people who accept the proposal with enthusiasm; it is *very rare* for a man to refuse categorically even though subsequently this has had an adverse effect on his life. I would give such a man full credit for his courage. Even KGB officers commend such men in official conversations among themselves.

In two months, I recruited eight agents of Soviet nationality in the unit and thereby fulfilled my task to the letter. I had failed in only one respect: I had not recruited any agents among the German community. Sometimes Boychenko reproached me for this. I endeavoured to use my ignorance of the German language as an excuse.

On one occasion, he told me that he personally would like to help me in the task of recruiting Germans. "I have got a good candidate for you," he said, "a German and a Russian speaker who is in touch with Soviet military personnel; he knows many of the residents in Bernau. Take a look at him, he is bound to be a good agent in the future."

After this recommendation, I set about studying the man, who can be called K, aged about 56. He was married, had a grown-up son, and devoted all his time to working for his family, to which he was extremely dutiful. He was one of the small band of GDR citizens who had remained in private business. He owned a small workshop in Bernau where he and his son repaired radio and television sets. They were both good craftsmen and worked hard, so their workshop brought in a considerable profit which enabled them to live well with their own house and three cars. Many people in Bernau jokingly nicknamed them "socialist capitalists". Indeed, living conditions being what they are in GDR, or for that matter in any other socialist country, the ordinary worker in a state enterprise cannot own three cars; very few are able to buy even one (which has to last many years) and then only with the help of relatives in most cases.

It is understandable that K was an unpleasant phenomenon for the local authorities of the Bernau region. His un-socialist life-style conflicted with Party ideology and official propaganda. His example subjected those around him to a "bourgeois influence". Party workers, therefore, created many difficulties for him, trying thereby to force him to give up his private workshop and compel him to work in a state enterprise like all other citizens.

The government could simply have banned all private businessmen, including K, and forbidden them to own their own enterprises, but it took the view that this would be an incorrect solution, since a veto of that sort would signify an inherent admission of the advantages of the capitalist way of life. So the authorities strove, by various means, to compel the few self-employed craftsmen to close their small shops and workshops and thus, in some measure, demonstrate to the simple "worker" the power of Socialism. They imposed increased taxes (surtax) on private businessmen and created obstacles for them in the procurement of goods, and so on.

For me, it was a great advantage that K was in private business. Indeed, it was subsequently possible to use this as a means of forcing him to work for us when the time came to recruit him.

It took me a month or so to get to know him well: to compile a detailed personality description from information I received from many agents who knew him, and also from the police of the GDR. Establishing contact with a German candidate for recruitment is a far from simple matter. As distinct from Soviet citizens, such a candidate must not know in the initial phase of cultivation that he is doing business with the KGB. Therefore any sort of plausible pretext is chosen to make his acquantaince which will allow a natural development of the contact, but disguise its real meaning.

In K's case, I decided to kick off with a radio ploy. I searched around for an old damaged transistor and then arrived with it at the workshop. I was in luck: K appeared in person, not his son, to take my instructions. I spoke to him in Russian. In the course of the conversation, K expressed an interest in what I was doing in the GDR. I replied, of course, that I was an infantry officer in the Soviet Army. K concluded the conversation by telling me that my radio would be repaired and ready to collect in a week's time.

And so the first get-together was now behind me, but I still had to find an excuse for further contacts. I found in a radio magazine a diagram for a high-power television aerial and I took it along to K at the workshop. I collected my radio which was ready, and then I put a further request: could he perhaps help me in the construction of a special television aerial? I showed him the diagram. K studied it and then promised to build it for me, remarking that there would be two to three weeks' delay since he did not have any suitable materials at the moment. His reply delighted me; it gave me an opportunity of paying him several further visits over the next two to three weeks.

Several days later, around six o'clock in the evening, when I knew that K's son was usually out after dinner delivering orders to customers, I appeared once again at the workshop. K greeted me as though we were already old friends, but told me that unfortunately my aerial was still being built. I thanked him for not having forgotten my request, glanced at my watch and suggested to him: "You know, it is long past work-time; if you have no objection, I would like to offer you some small token of my thanks in the Russian style for your endeavours. I have a small surprise for you, some Russian vodka from Moscow! "

"Oh, these Russians," chuckled K, "they will always find an excuse for a party! " He closed up his workshop and placed two glasses on the table. I fished out the vodka bottle from my briefcase and we began to chat. He was interested in how people lived in Russia and I put a variety of questions about life in the GDR, his family and his work. The conversation was a lively one and the time flashed by. Each of us was well pleased with this conversation. As we bade each other farewell, K invited me to call any evening. "I would not like to remain in your debt; we Germans also know how to entertain."

"Fine," I agreed, "I will come without fail."

And so, little by little, I established close and cordial relations. During several further meetings I tried to conduct the conversation in a way that would encourage him to talk more about his acquaintances. He described their characteristics and, not suspecting my sinister designs, gave me a thorough and frank account of his friends, acquaintances and problems at home. He came to regret this later.

About a month after this, Boychenko summoned me to find out how the preparations were going. When I had reported, he announced that the time had come to recruit K, and we decided to effect this the following Saturday in one of the "safe" houses.

On Wednesday, I called on K and invited him to my house on Saturday "to improve our acquaintance and strengthen our friendship." He was agreeable, and I said I would come by car at two o'clock to collect him. On the Saturday, we set off together for my home—the "safe" flat—where Boychenko was waiting. "You have got a fine Saturday ahead of you, K," I mused to myself. "You will have a lot to go through."

The flat was in the suburbs of Bernau in one of a number of insignificant little houses screened by a garden from the gaze of passers by. "So you are not too badly set up," remarked K as we drove up to the house. "I was not expecting a junior infantry officer to live so well." "The unexpected is only just beginning," I said as a joke, the real meaning of which K only understood later.

We went indoors and I led K into a room where there was a table already laid and, of course, Boychenko. "My boss," I said, "Lieutenant-Colonel Ivanov. He also wants to celebrate a little with us."

Boychenko extended a hand to K and invited him to sit down. "I am very glad to make your acquaintance, I have heard a lot about you." "Andrey [the name by which K knew me] has often talked to me about you," said K hesitantly. It was obvious that he had no understanding of what was happening.

"Never mind," Boychenko began, "we shall have time enough today to get to know each other. I see that you don't quite understand what it is all about; Andrey obviously forgot to tell you that he is an officer of the KGB."

"KGB!" exclaimed a horrified K.

"Of course," Boychenko rejoined casually.

"But why are you telling me all this, I don't want to know anything at all about it. I thought that I was invited as a friend to Andrey's home. What's the KGB doing here?"

"Now please don't upset yourself," soothed Boychenko. "We shall explain everything to you. We just have a few questions to put to you and I think that we can resolve them together quite successfully."

K endeavoured to say something but Boychenko, excusing himself, went on: "We have had you under observation for a long time. You are a very interesting chap, astute, you have interesting connections and considerable experience of life. We would like to become friends with you. We need people like you. In other words, we are suggesting that you co-operate with us. You could render us some small services and, of course, you will not remain out of pocket."

This was recruitment by the direct method, "on the forehead" as the KGB calls it, and it was the right one: K was an astute man and it was better not to beat about the bush. He reacted violently. "Under no circumstances! I will never give my agreement to it. I think that any further conversation on the subject is pointless." With these words he stood up, giving us to understand that the conversation was at an end.

"Don't be in such a hurry," Boychenko interrupted coldly. "Our chat is only just beginning and I think that you would be better advised not to rush over your answers and actions."

K clearly understood that it was not so simple to disentangle himself from the KGB and sank back into an armchair.

"I shall try to explain to you briefly and simply some unalterable things," Boychenko said in harsh tones. "We are struggling with our enemies in the defence of Socialism, not just the USSR but the entire Socialist camp. Therefore, every *genuine* [he particularly stressed this word] citizen of the Socialist camp whom we ask to collaborate with us is under an obligation to help us. In other words he who is not with us is against us."

The explanation was simple but effective. Indeed, if someone being recruited were to say "No" then indirectly he would put himself in the ranks of the unreliable and "non-genuine". Despite this, K made one further attempt to refuse, exploiting such arguments as his age, the state of his health and so on.

Boychenko switched to open threats and blackmail. "We have no desire to speak to you about unpleasant things but you force me to do so. So then, if you refuse to collaborate, we shall act as follows: firstly we shall compromise you. I hope that you have not forgotten that you spent some time talking to Andrey about your acquaintances and friends, and described them to him. Andrey recorded some of what you told him on a tape recorder. We have the possibility, armed with this tape, of persuading certain of your acquaintances that you have been collaborating for a long time with the KGB. If this were to happen, it seems to me that life in Bernau might not be very pleasant for you. Secondly, as I understand it, you possess a private workshop?" "Yes." "And that son of yours is hoping to study in university?" "Yes."

"Well then, you know that we are in a position to ruin everything." The colonel mercilessly hammered K on his most painful spot. "You will lose your workshop, your son will never study in university. As you see, the future of your family and its welfare lies in your hands. Well now, what are you going to say in answer to our proposal, yes or no?"

All this time I had kept my eyes on K. His face was pale. Beads of sweat trickled down his forehead, his hands were shaking. He understood that he had no way out. He had to decide today, this very moment, the fate of his family. "Yes," he groaned from somewhere within himself.

"Well now, that puts things in a different light. I knew we would see eye to eye," Boychenko replied approvingly and cynically.

K signed a document in which he expressed his *voluntary* agreement to co-operate. He worked subsequently under the pseudonym Stefan. When his recruitment was complete, K was invited to partake of a glass of vodka to celebrate, but he complained of a headache and refused, so I took him home. He spent the next two weeks in hospital with heart trouble.

That is a sample of how the KGB recruits its agents in the GDR. It affects not only Soviet and GDR citizens, but also some citizens of West Germany and other capitalist states who visit that country.

The two recruitment cases described above are average, run-of-the-mill occurrences in the work of the KGB. But more complicated cases do, of course, occur in which recruitment is prepared over a longer period. In such cases all the circumstances surrounding a forthcoming recruitment are determined. The basis is carefully prepared in what way, and with the application of which measures, a particular individual is to be forced to co-operate.

Such long drawn out preparations are required most often for visitors from capitalist countries, since the prerequisites for recruitment are totally different from those which apply in the case of Soviet or GDR citizens. As such people are neither directly nor indirectly dependent on the KGB, the organisation has to resort to rather more ruses and conducts itself more cautiously. However, the basic principles still remain the same: bribery, threats or blackmail.

The recruitment of a woman from Stuttgart by the name of N was one example. From 1966 onwards, she had visited relatives on several occasions in Bad Grünwald in the GDR. The KGB, who as usual were checking the arrival lists of Westerners, took an interest in her. They decided to exploit her for the information she could provide on West Germany. An agent made her acquaintance, as it were, "by chance". He established a very close relationship with romantic overtones, and later introduced her to a "friend", a KGB officer. The "friend" referred to the difficulties of pronouncing her real name and called her Mariya. "Better and simpler," he explained. At one of their meetings, the agent handed over to N an expensive present on behalf of his absent friend and asked her to write a note of thanks to his address. N, quite unsuspectingly, wrote the following note to the "friend": "Thank you for your valuable present. I am very pleased. Mariya."

The KGB intended to use this note as a form of blackmail in N's recruitment. Indeed, the contents of the note were very similar to an agent's receipt working under the pseudonym "Mariya" who had just received a reward for a task she had executed. All this provided an opportunity, in the event of N being stubborn, of forcing her to co-operate by threatening to compromise her and to expose her to the West Germans as a KGB agent.

Several days later the "friend" himself turned up on N's doorstep with the note. N thanked him for the present. Then the "friend" declared himself to be an employee of the KGB and suggested that she should co-operate, promising a good reward. With much hesitation, N replied in the affirmative; a speedy acknowledgement of the efficacy of KGB blackmail and threats.

Although the recruitment of agents certainly plays an important part in the KGB's work, it is not the principal factor. The main one is to force recruited agents to work productively, to hand over vital intelligence so as to guarantee a successful outcome to the KGB's activities.

CHAPTER 8

Creating enemies to "unmask"

THE secret service has to give visible and tangible results on behalf of the state which it serves. The KGB is the child of the Soviet Communist régime, "the shield and sword" of the state. For this reason, all its activity should be viewed as part of the activity of the régime directed towards its defence, preservation and reinforcement. An everyday requirement is that it should work "more productively", amassing more "positive" results against enemies of the state; it is unimportant whether they are internal or external.

Counter-espionage is a fruitful field for gaining "positive" results. For the sake of objectivity, it must be noted that sometimes these results include real counter-espionage successes, but in the majority of cases they are invented in response to the demands made in the "glorious" fight against the enemies of Communism. During my work I had occasion to see both sides. I shall begin by relating a genuine success.

Soon after my arrival in the Department in 1969, I was fortunate enough to participate in an operation to unmask a real spy network concerned in collecting information about Soviet troops. One of the many MfS informers, a woman, reported that GDR citizen Rodiger, who then lived in Bernau, kept certain mysterious chemical substances at his home. She was instructed to steal some of these substances. When they were analysed, it was discovered that they could be used to prepare secret texts. Rodiger was put under close observation. Soon it was established that, under various pretexts, he often turned up near military emplacements and sometimes, under the pretext of buying goods, even in Soviet shops, and he visited Soviet military units.

All this information was promptly handed over by MfS to Soviet counter-espionage, i.e. to the KGB Special Department in Bernau where, at that time, I was working. The KGB went straight to work. From that day onwards every step Rodiger took was watched by both the KGB and MfS. Hidden observation posts were set up around all Soviet units and they noted every appearance Rodiger made near an encampment. His personality was carefully studied. All his connections came to light and were noted down. At the same time, all his relations were checked. After two or three months of such activity, it was finally established that he worked for one of the Western espionage agencies. To collect information on Soviet units, he had drawn in his relations as well, and altogether seven people were implicated.

The security forces began to prepare for their arrest. Proof was collected that Rodiger and his relations were gathering information about Soviet units which Rodiger himself was handing over to the West. Photographs were obtained showing Rodiger and his relations in the act of observing troop movements, and of his meeting with his relations and giving them espionage tasks. Finally, all was ready for the arrest of the network. The operation was to be carried out by MfS. This procedure is followed to hide to some extent the activity of the KGB in the GDR and in order to underline yet again the fictitious "independence" of the East German régime.

It was decided that the arrests should be carried out secretly in September 1969, so that their friends, neighbours and those relations still at liberty should know nothing about it for several days. Ambushes were to be laid at the flats of those arrested and left for several days in case any of the accomplices still unknown to the KGB and MfS turned up. Everything happened as planned. One night all seven people were arrested. The ambushes left behind in their flats produced nothing. All were interrogated by MfS, in the presence of KGB officers. Rodiger confessed that he had been working for the French for about 14 years. He behaved bravely; accepted the main guilt personally and tried to produce evidence to lessen the guilt of his relations. At the trial, he was condemned to life imprisonment, his relations to various terms of imprisonment. The event was solemny celebrated in our Department as a great success, and many of its workers were promoted. Boychenko, as head of the Department, was awarded an "honourable mention" by KGB Chairman Andropov.

However, unmasking Western agents is a rare occurrence although the demand for results is never ending, each quarter, each half year, each year. Those workers who cannot produce results are considered either as inept or as having lost their "political vigilance", and therefore not showing the necessary élan. I would say that it is almost impossible for such workers to make a career in the KGB; they are constantly criticised and sent to work in distant regions such as the Trans Baikal, the Far North. They do not receive promotion at the due time, and for this reason, every worker tries to produce results. And where can these most easily be achieved? In the struggle against internal enemies, of course. While it is difficult to catch a spy—the majority of counter-espionage workers have seen them only on the cinema screens—there is no lack of "anti-Soviets" and other "internal enemies" of the régime. They are to be found everywhere: you need only take a close look to find them. It is with their help that a career can be made.

I recall how the conference called to assess the year's results was conducted in the Department in 1970. General Titov, head of the Directorate of Special Departments of the KGB in the GDR, and other high-ranking officers attended. Each officer, beginning with our chief, Boychenko, had to report. The results were far from brilliant and the big chiefs were not pleased. In his summing up, General Titov criticised us sharply and demanded that we increase our active work. Of all he said, it was the following phrases which remained in my mind, as it is a fair description of the KGB's counter-espionage activities:

"I fully understand that it is difficult to catch spies. There are, after all, few of them. And not one of them comes himself and says, 'I am a spy'. But we must get to work. So if there are no spies, then you must unmask anti-Soviets and other internal enemies. They are always to be found and if you can't find any, then create them."

The request was plain for all to see, if there are no spies then "create" anti-Soviets and other enemies of the régime. This was not difficult as every Soviet citizen who was even slightly dissatisfied could, given the desire, be transformed into a violent enemy of Communism and of the Soviet régime. And to unmask such an enemy is really a result. However phoney, such an "unmasking" means rewards and the recognition of a career by the powers that be. Internal enemies are still enemies.

In 1970, I was implicated in the affair of an internal enemy, a lieutenant-colonel of the army I shall call Ko. At the time Ko was serving in the military hospital of the 20th Guards Regiment at Bad-Frenenwald. He was the doctor in charge of the X-ray room. Captain Tarasov of the Bernau KGB was responsible for that hospital. One of his informers, a private also serving in the hospital, told Tarasov that he accidentally heard Ko talking to officers of the hospital. According to the private, Ko was criticising the electoral system in the USSR, saying that they were purely formal as there was really no one to elect, except one candidate appointed by the Party leadership. And anyway what kind of elections could exist if the country had only *one* Party? He compared elections in the USSR with a theatrical performance. In spite of the fact that Ko's words corresponded to reality and were objective, they were considered to be anti-Soviet. This is understandable under the prevailing conditions for according to official propaganda, the USSR is the most democratic country in the world. A Ko dossier, with the title of "demagogue" was immediately started, as well as an active check and re-check of his activities. One of his officer friends was recruited as an agent to collect evidence showing him to be anti-Soviet. Ko trusted this agent, and most of their conversations were listened in to and tape-recorded. It emerged from all the material received, that Ko was in full agreement with a Communist régime. The only thing he wanted was a multi-party system under Communism. And so, he was no enemy of Communism, but in the KGB's opinion he had fallen for a hostile ideology and so had become a dangerous social element.

"He probably listens to radio transmissions from the Voice of America and Radio Free Europe," Boychenko remarked. This itself was dangerous. It was also considered dangerous that Ko had expressed his opinions aloud, and that although these were, in fact, not anti-Soviet, they were nevertheless dangerous. Bearing in mind that he was a distinguished officer who took part in the war, it was decided not to take him to court. But he was transferred back to the USSR and subsequently relieved of his army post. That was how our Department unmasked yet another enemy, although this time only a "potential enemy".

At the end of 1972, the KGB received an order from Andropov to activate still further its works against citizens of Jewish nationality. There were very few Jews in units of the 6th Guards Motorised Rifle Division for which we were operationally responsible in connection with the law forbidding them to serve abroad. As a rule, they were officers' wives. After receipt of Andropov's order, we were immediately instructed to check all Jews yet again and, if at all possible, find a reason for sending them back to the USSR.

There was only one Jewess, Birasten Lyudmilla Viktorovna, in the 16th Motorised Rifle Regiment for which I was at that time responsible. Her husband was a senior lieutenant who had served in the regiment for about two years. I had no negative reports at all on either her or her husband. After a week, I reported to my chief, Lieutenant-Colonel Strizhenko (Boychenko had by this time been promoted and transferred to Moscow) that all was in order.

"Aleksei Alekseevich, that is no solution to the problem," retorted Strizhenko. "All is in order! It is impossible at the present time for all to be in order with Jews. You must find something. We must remove her from the GDR in not less than one month."

At heart I was disgusted, but did not dare disobey. Gradually I began to look for "something" against Birasten. The only thing I found was that she kept up a friendship with a German woman, a shop assistant, in Bad-Frenenwald and that she sometimes visited Berlin without prior permission. I reported this to Strizhenko. "That's another matter altogether," he said, rubbing his hands. "Now we can tip her and her husband out of the GDR."

"What for?" I asked.

"What do you mean, what for? When she knows a German

woman, a shop assistant, it means a clear case of speculation. Does she herself travel to Berlin without permission? She does, which is an infringement of the rules of behaviour for Soviet citizens posted abroad. Of course, in itself that is not enough. In addition to that, we must find something if only slightly anti-Soviet, say, a desire to go to Israel. What do you think?" He looked at me questioningly and then added: "I'll tell you what. We will call her into the Department and get her written confession that she is speculating and visits Berlin illegally and that, at the same time, she would like to go to Israel. And then that will be another positive result for our work. It will be of use to everyone, to you as a good worker, to me as your chief and even to Birasten herself because after that we will leave her alone."

An order is an order and it was quite a normal one for the KGB, that "Office of Crude Bandits" to which I belonged. Next day, Birasten was called to the Special Department for a chat which Strizhenko himself conducted in my presence. It was full of threats, promises, flattery etc. The scene was disgusting. Even now, when I recall it all, I feel sick at heart. In a short while, her husband and Birasten were sent to serve in the Far East of the USSR and for the KGB it meant the successful conclusion of yet another "complex operation".

Another incident occurred at the end of 1973 and the beginning of 1974. Major Strizhenko, at 36, was still young to occupy the post of head of a department. For that reason, he tried to justify his appointment by achieving extra successes. All hope lay in "internal enemies" who could always be "created". At that time, I had been working in the Department for five years and was considered an experienced worker. I was then a captain. My career was not built on "anti-Soviets". I had simply been lucky; I was concerned in the unmasking of Rodiger. I was concerned in espionage. Also I was a kind of expert in recruitment; as a rule, agents recruited by me worked actively and provided valuable information. Strizhenko behaved towards me with respect and, if we were alone, we talked not as a chief and a subordinate, but as equals.

At the beginning of 1973, I recruited Lieutenant Shibunko, an officer of the 16th Motorised Rifle Regiment as an agent. His code name was "Skiba", and he proved to be one of those agents who co-operate with real pleasure. It was obvious that it gave him great satisfaction to furnish the KGB with written reports about others, perhaps because he gained a feeling of power. On each occasion when he met me, he tried to report something "black" about his colleagues, acquaintances and friends. Around September 1973, I received from him a written report to the effect that one officer of the regiment,

Lieutenant Smirnov, occasionally listened to Radio Free Europe. When asked by "Skiba" why he did it, Smirnov replied that he wished to have a complete account of world events, whereas our newspapers did not always report everything.

Information is information, and I, at first, did not attach any particular attention to it. Just think, some lieutenant or other sometimes listens to Radio Free Europe. Of course in the USSR it is considered an anti-Soviet station, although the fact that Smirnov occasionally listened to it did not prove that he was an enemy of the state. Many citizens secretly listen to these transmissions with the sole aim of hearing true reports. Some accounts in Soviet newspapers distort world events and describe them in a favourable light insofar as the Communist régime is concerned, and some events are not even reported at all.

But it was out of the question for me not to act on "Skiba's" information about Smirnov; every written report is registered, the KGB officer who receives it, must give his written opinion of its content, work out what measures he intends to take and report to his chief that the information has been received.

On the basis of "Skiba's" report, I gave a negative appraisal of Smirnov's behaviour, although I did not consider it dangerous for the régime. I suggested that the appropriate action would be to inform the deputy regimental commander responsible for political work, who would have a chat with Smirnov. Next day, Strizhenko came to see me carrying my recommendation. "Aleksei Alekseevich," he began in an excited voice: "What we need are actions with a future, leading to results, results. And what are you doing?"

"What?" I did not understand what he meant.

"I'll tell you this minute what!" He took the report from his briefcase. "Such a report. And you evaluate it as insignificant. I did not expect it of you. Smirnov is a hidden enemy. I order you to undertake a close check of him."

"It will all be in vain, we will not achieve any result at all here; Smirnov is a normal Soviet citizen," I objected.

"Aleksei Alekseevich," said Strizhenko, employing a less official tone, "do not forget that we need the results of unmasking. Therefore, we must make Smirnov into an enemy. I personally shall concern myself with him, along with you, of course." Thereupon he put before me a plan. "Skiba" was to gain Smirnov's confidence by being a kindred soul. Then, he must provoke Smirnov into a political discussion and make him pronounce some negative opinions about the system in the USSR. It was planned to tape-record what was said. "And that is how we shall make an anti-Soviet out of him," Strizhenko concluded.

I briefed "Skiba", and Strizhenko and I waited to see whether he would gain Smirnov's confidence. I doubted it as they were complete opposites. One of them was by nature an informer, a Shpik, an agent provocateur, or as they are called "Seksot" (secret collaborator). The other was an honest open-hearted, thinking chap. As I expected, "Skiba" was unable to work up a relationship: so Strizhenko's first plan failed.

A week later, Strizhenko came to me with a new plan. He suggested recruiting one of Smirnov's own friends as an agent. After much deliberation, Strizhenko and I settled on Smirnov's close friend, a junior doctor in the regiment, Lieutenant Telinger. The fact that he was a clever and intelligent chap spoke in his favour. He was respected by his colleagues. He liked to enjoy himself. He was not interested in politics and most important of all, he often spent his free time in the company of Smirnov. It remained an open question whether Telinger would co-operate to work against Smirnov. Here Strizhenko placed all his faith in me. "You are an expert in such matters, Aleksei Alekseevich. You must recruit him and prepare him for work. I take the remaining work upon myself."

I recruited Telinger in a couple of weeks. He was given the code name "Sedoi" (grey) and a week later, he set to work. He engaged Smirnov in heart-to-heart discussions and gradually introduced a political tone, provoking him into making so-called anti-Soviet remarks by himself making careful criticism of the régime. Having noticed that in Telinger, he had found a like-minded colleague, Smirnov, in his innocence, readily discussed with him the government's internal policies.

A considerable amount of material had been accumulated by the end of January 1974. In chatting with "Sedoi", Smirnov had said that there was no true democracy in the USSR, and that he did not like the one-party system which excluded any kind of democracy. He compared the work of the KGB with the Inquisition, and those persecuted in the USSR with "heretics" who, in the majority of cases, suffered only on account of their convictions. According to Smirnov, the KGB was even worse than the Inquisition, which more often than not destroyed its victims physically, whereas the KGB first attempted to destroy the spirit and morale of an individual and only afterwards, if necessary, subjected his body to labour camp, prison or deportation.

Strizhenko rubbed his hands in delight when he received all this material, confirmed by tape-recordings. "Well, what did I tell you, Aleksei Alekseevich, he is an enemy, a real enemy! Now we only have to prove and arrange for him to be found organising an anti-Soviet group and then we can put him safely away in prison for a long time. And that would be a good result! "

As I listened, I was thinking of very different things. Smirnov was speaking the truth as I myself knew after years of work in the KGB. At that time, I was a long way away from its aims in my convictions, and I was already taking concrete measures to make my personal contribution to the struggle against the Cheka and against Communism. The Smirnov case was not finished when on 2 February 1974 I found myself in the West. Smirnov, I hope, remained free. But that is how enemies of the régime are made out of innocent people and later sent to camps and prisons.

The search for enemies is carried out not only through KGB informers but also through the public. KGB officers often make public speeches and lectures about the black deeds of Western espionage agencies, thus artificially creating a psychosis among the population and calling for all-round vigilance. One example, taken from my personal experience, shows clearly to what such spy-mania can lead.

I worked alongside KGB agent "Petrov" (his real name was Malashevich), an army major in the 16th Motorised Rifle Regiment. He was an active collaborator, fulfilling many assignments, and as a result often had to be away from home on various pretexts. Naturally, his wife did not like this. She wanted to know where he went when others were sitting at home, and where the money which he had from time to time came from. Malashevich was strictly forbidden to tell his wife that he collaborated with the KGB and continuously had to invent various reasons, some of which sometimes sounded rather far fetched. He often quarrelled with his wife about this, but always as a family quarrel, until one day. . . .

One day, someone knocked at my office door and in came Malashevich's wife. This was quite unexpected. However, I did not show it. I offered her a chair and asked her what had brought her to see me.

"Not long ago, I listened to you talk on vigilance," she began with a shaking voice. "I thought a great deal about it and finally decided to come and see you." It was obvious that she was very upset. I tried to calm her and asked her what was worrying her. She burst into tears, then said: "I think my husband is a spy, he is connected with some Americans or English people."

I expected anything, but not that. Perhaps I had heard her wrongly. "A spy?" "Yes, a spy."

"That is a serious accusation," I said severely. "What has led you to that supposition?"

"I shall explain everything. You know my husband is often away from home, he goes away somewhere or other and is permanently in a state of nerves. Something is wrong with him. I know there is no other woman, he cannot even sleep with me. Then there is the money."

"What money?" I asked.

"You know what it is like in a family, I always check my husband's pockets and I always find money there, not much, 50 marks or 100 marks, but it is always there. And you see, he gives me all his wages to the last penny. Where does he get the extra money from? And so I have been thinking that perhaps he is a spy? He works at head-quarters with secret documents."

It was obvious to me. Malashevich's work for me explained his absences and the money. But I did not hurry, because I was interested. Sitting before me was a woman who had lived 17 years with her husband, raised two children with him and yet she had come volun-tarily with serious accusations against him. What had made her take such a step? Jealousy, hatred or the desire to get rid of her husband?

"Do you understand what you are accusing your husband of?" "Yes."

"Think again, perhaps you are mistaken," I suggested. "I have already thought about it a great deal."

"So what now then?" "I've already told you that. I think he may be a spy."

"What is your relationship with your husband? Do you often quarrel with him? Perhaps you do not understand each other? Or alternatively, perhaps there is another man?"

"No, I love my husband and do not forget that he is the father of my children but, before all else I am a Communist and I tell you there is something wrong with him."

"Right," I said. "Can you give me a written statement?" I offered her pen and paper. She agreed and wrote down the details.

I took the written statement from her; locked it in my safe, unhurriedly lit a cigarette and after some thought, I asked: "What do you think will happen to your husband now?"

"I do not know."

"And what if we arrest him?"

"If my husband is a spy, then he deserves it."

"A firm reply," I thought and decided to stop it all. "Listen to me carefully. Your husband is not a spy. He is a KGB collaborator. He fulfills the tasks we set him, that is why he has to be away from home and we give him money for his expenses."

"My husband collaborates with you, and I thought he was a spy!" she exclaimed with relief.

"Never mind, it happens," I said. "Thank you for the courageous step you took today. By that you have shown that you are a true

Communist. That is how it should always be, the Party first and then private life."

These high-sounding phrases meant nothing and I pronounced them with the secret hope that she would perhaps see the irony of it all. But she took my remarks seriously with a thankful expression. Having revealed that her husband was a collaborator, I had to recruit her also to keep the secret and make sure of using Malashevich in the future. She readily agreed and assured me that she would make every effort to help the KGB, which, even without her assurance, I did not doubt for one moment.

Then, remembering her poor husband, she asked me not to tell him that she had accused him of being a spy. I assured her that it was strictly between us and ushered her out. Left alone, I took her statement from the safe and tore it into small pieces. Such is life where a spy-mania psychosis reigns.

It is a well-known fact that the KGB does not always "create" enemies and that sometimes Chekists prefer to deal with "madmen". An example was Private Golubev. Of course, his case cannot even be compared with that of General Grigorenko, but a mere private is also a human being. In 1972, he was serving in the 16th Motorised Rifle Regiment of the 6th Motorised Rifle Division. For a long time, there was no difference between him and the others until one day an incident occurred during political study.

His platoon commander, Lieutenant Melder, was telling his soldiers of the advantages of Communism over capitalism and about the bright Communist future. When he finished speaking, Private Golubev suddenly jumped up and cried:

"Comrade Lieutenant, I do not agree with you, I consider that the life of an ordinary worker in America is better than in our country. How do you explain that?" The other soldiers waited curiously to hear the lieutenant's reply. He said that Golubev was mistaken and ordered him to be quiet. After the political study period, he sent him to talk to the deputy head of the Political Department, Major Konik.

Major Konik's attempts to compel Golubev to change his mind failed. Golubev obstinately stuck to his opinion and even suggested to Konik that he should hold a discussion with his soldiers on that subject. The major put Golubev in the guardroom and sent a report to the KGB. Strizhenko informed me as I was responsible for the regiment, and on my advice, he decided not to take repressive measures against Golubev, because the other soldiers knew what had happened. He "advised" the head of the Political Department of the 6th Guards Division, Colonel Chelyshev, to send Golubev for observation to the Psychiatric Department of the hospital in Topitz, where he was to be pronounced "mentally deranged".

Golubev was taken straight from the guardroom to the hospital, where appropriately briefed doctors awaited him. In a couple of weeks he was pronounced "ill" and sent to the USSR, where he was demobilised. It was explained to the soldiers who had witnessed the incident that mental illness accounted for his "abnormal" views.

I have recounted only a little of the work of a small department. If one looks at the activities of the KGB as a whole, then the few examples I have quoted make it possible to imagine how many "enemies" have been "created" throughout the USSR. These "enemies" now sit in prisons and camps, and how many more "mentally ill" people are undergoing forced "medical" treatment?

CHAPTER 9

The privileged ones

SOVIET citizens have to live under laws created by the Communist régime and with a myriad of regulations. Offenders may be imprisoned in a prison or labour camp, lose a good job or be forbidden to attend an institute and so on. A particularly comprehensive list of regulations exists for citizens living abroad, irrespective of whether they belong to the army or are private citizens.

For example, army personnel as well as civilians living in East Germany are forbidden to make "free" unorganised contacts with its citizens, even though they are brothers in class, conviction and arms. Officers, privates and their families are strictly forbidden to leave the confines of the garrison where they are serving. Visits to West Berlin are especially forbidden. It is considered particularly dangerous as many foreigners from capitalist countries: Americans, British, French and West Berlin citizens, Federal German nationals, are permanently based there, and this could lead to undesirable contacts. The KGB is also afraid that Soviet citizens may be recruited by some Western agency or even that they may try to flee to the West. Military commanders and Party leaders alike are afraid of such contacts, as they fear the influence of "bourgeois ideology".

But most of these prohibitions are intended for the mass of ordinary folk. How then do those in power and those who defend that power live? How do KGB agents live, for example—those who are the "sword and shield" of Soviet power? It would seem that in fulfilling their duty of defending and strengthening the Soviet régime, they must be among the most convinced Communists. So they are; but they believe in their own brand of Communism, belonging as they do to the Soviet élite, to its "Mafia".

For this "Mafia", Communism is quite a different proposition from the one known to the simple worker; it means unlimited power over the masses, a secure life at other peoples' expense and all-embracing rules and discipline: that is the kind of barrack-square Communism in which Chekists believe. To the workers, Communists promise a bright future with happiness, brotherhood and equality for all, but they do not say when this will be achieved. The people compare Communism to an elusive horizon—"the more effort spent to get closer, the quicker the horizon moves into the distance".

KGB workers have more freedom in their personal lives than other citizens; they wield enormous power and enjoy total control of the citizens, to whom they appear impregnable. For this reason, they are more uninhibited when considering political problems as well; they are often uncomplimentary in their remarks about individual Soviet leaders and about the internal and external polices of the government. Yet one rule is strictly adhered to: all opinions and remarks must not go beyond the confines of the KGB. This represents a sort of unwritten privilege and is explained by the well-known phrase: "What is permissible to Jupiter is forbidden to the bull." They are truly the most privileged of the Communist New Class or Soviet bourgeoisie.

While talking with colleagues, I often heard the most varied opinions about one or another government official, including Brezhnev himself. He was sharply criticised for the "softness" of his internal policies and for his mistakes in external policy. However, it must be said that on the whole the KGB approves of him; over the past few years, he has widened and strengthened the rights and power of the KGB. He has given more privileges to Cheka men; increased their pay and allotted more funds to the KGB as a whole. "He's not as stupid as Khruschev was," said Colonel Spirin, head of the Special Department of the KGB attached to the 20th Guards Army. "He understands that one cannot do without the KGB."

Other Politburo members come in for their share of criticism. Chekists are particularly contemptuous about Kunaev. They reproach him for his drunkenness and idleness, and refer to him as a useless member of the government. Conversations among KGB workers refer particularly cynically to political freedoms in the USSR or to such organisations as "trade unions" and "local Soviets". These exist only as a façade to impress the world and they play hardly any real role at all. KGB people know all this better than anyone, and among themselves refer to these organisations as "shop windows". As regards the state structure, insofar as its "freedoms" and "democracies" are concerned, KGB men often relate anecdotes for which an ordinary mortal would immediately be sentenced under the Article "Slander against the Soviet state and social order". There is one such anecdote.

The son of a highly-placed Party official did not work well at school. He had particular difficulty studying the state structure. He could not get into his head the significance of different conceptions like the Party, the Motherland, trade unions and the people. Not wishing that his own authority should suffer, the father decided to teach his son himself. For two whole hours, he unsuccessfully tried to teach his son what Party, Motherland and people meant. All was in vain; his son did not understand. Then the father decided to use practical methods. "Well," he said, "I am the Party, your mother is the Motherland, your grandmother is the trade unions and you are the people." And with the help of this illustration, he began to explain everything from the beginning. But the son still did not understand. Furious, the father put his son in the corner as a punishment for several hours. Later, he forgot about him. All this took place in the bedroom unfortunately. During the night, the father started to make love to his wife. Watching from his corner, the son remembered his grandmother asleep next door and thought to himself: "What a life! The Party rapes the Motherland, the trade unions sleep and the people have to suffer! "

At the Special Department of the KGB in Bernau, I had fairly quickly established friendly relations with many of its officers. Sometimes, after working hours, two or three of us joined up to visit the town cafes, or the officers' mess to play billiards, or else we met at someone's flat to have a glass of vodka, a chat and to criticise our chiefs. This was part of our daily lives on weekdays, but there are also public holidays: Revolution Day, the First of May, Victory Day and other celebrations. The officers of our Department in common with all other Chekists made the most of these festival dates, that is to say to organise official drinking bouts. KGB officers refer among themselves to such drunken orgies as "cultural-political measures" (abbreviated as KPM). Nobody knows where this ironic title originated, but it is a pretty fair description, firstly because these orgies are official events which give them a political character; secondly, they take place with the participation and under the leadership of the KGB chiefs. Before each glass a toast is obligatory, to the CPSU, the Government, the Politburo or to Brezhnev himself. Everyone must drain his glass. These bouts are all paid for from public funds; the working class is not short of money for its "servants". Never forget that the KGB *serves* the people!

My first experience of a KPM was on 23 February 1969, Soviet Army Day. A couple of days before, Lavrukhin and I sat in his room chatting. It was about nine in the evening. Suddenly, Koroteyev burst in in his usual tipsy state. "Why are you still working? You should be getting ready for the festivities."

"Who needs to prepare, we are always ready," answered Lavrukhin.

"You are ready, but who will organise the whole thing, good drinks and hors d'oeuvres? Koroteyev of course," Kostya continued. ' I have been to the head of the officers' mess and warned him. Everything will be first class."

Lavrukhin burst out laughing. "You like that job, organising drunken bouts." "Of course, it is better than working! I have not been home for two days and my wife will kill me! "

At about 8 p.m. on 23 February, we gathered in a room at the officers' mess where a table loaded with drinks and hors d'oeuvres was waiting. Most of us were in civilian clothes, it being less incongruous to see a civilian dead drunk. At the table the places of honour were occupied by Boychenko and Kryukov. I sat between Lavrukhin and Davydov. Boychenko rose, glass in hand, and delivered a short speech praising the Party, Brezhnev, the army and, of course, the KGB. The toast was promptly honoured.

In a couple of minutes, Kryukov toasted the KGB and its leadership, and we all drank to it readily. Then he added: "I suggest that each one of us proposing a toast should not spend longer than two minutes over it otherwise we shall not have enough time to drink! If anyone cannot manage in the time, he will be punished and will have to drink a 'fine'—200 grammes of vodka."

The proposal was wholeheartedly supported. Kostya Koroteyev shouted: "Aleksandr Gerasimovich! I stammer anyway and will not be able to manage in the time. So allow me to drink my 'fine' straight away!"

"I'll show you whether you'll drink a 'fine' or not," threatened Kryukov. "You must last out to the end of our drinking bout, otherwise, as usual, you will be under the table before it's over." Speeches were made, glasses emptied, spirits rose, here and there passions were rising It started with the chiefs.

A couple of days before the drinking session, there had been the usual quarrel between Boychenko and Kryukov, this time over the Department's interpreter, Lieutenant Nagishkin. He asked Boychenko for two days' leave and was refused. Then Nagishkin approached Kryukov, who sanctioned it. Boychenko made a scene, threatening to report the matter to "a higher authority" and even to punish Kryukov. Passions seemed to have calmed, but not, in his cups. Boychenko suddenly remembered it all. "Who is in charge, you or I?" he shouted in a drunken voice at Kryukov.

"You are a chief for them," said Kryukov, pointing to us, "but for me you are nothing more than . . . . !" (unprintable expression).

Boychenko grabbed Kryukov and began to shake him. With difficulty we managed to separate them. The drinking continued. Soon the losses became apparent. Davydov was first, and a driver was called to take him home. Leaning on the private's shoulder and singing his favourite song, 'When the evening lights are swaying', Davydov left the happy company. Zemskov and Koroteyev were the next to disappear, they went to Berlin to "look for women". Having forgotten his quarrel with Boychenko, Kryukov sat embracing one of the maids and shortly afterwards they left together.

Lavrukhin and I also wanted to go home but Boychenko said: "We shall all go to the Department together. I want to speak to

Nagishkin again officially and you must be present." To the Department the man said, so the Department it is. The four of us, Boychenko, Nagishkin, Lavrukhin and I, got into a car and arrived in about ten minutes. Boychenko's conversation with Nagishkin took place outside. Swaying from side to side, he approached Nagishkin saying: "Am I the chief or am I not?" "The chief," the latter replied. "Why the hell don't you listen to me then instead of running to Kryukov? I'll punch your face in for it this very minute." He took a swing at Nagishkin, who, however, was only half as tall as Boychenko, and the blow missed. Boychenko lost his balance and lay spreadeagled on the ground with a bloody face. He struggled to his feet; tried to hit Nagishkin again, but again fell and lay in the snow. We lifted him up, brushed off the snow and drove him home. There we placed him outside the front door; rang the bell and immediately left as we were afraid of his wife's reaction. That was the end of my first "cultural-political measure".

Such KPMs were a regular occurrence in the Department. Sometimes they went off smoothly, but sometimes strange things happened. I recall how, at one such drunken bout, Boychenko and Kryukov actually did fight. Although it was a short contest because neither could stand properly, they managed to damage each other's faces so badly that neither could appear for a week to the great amusement of all the other officers. These fights provided material for all manner of jokes among their subordinates, who, of course, did scarcely any work while Boychenko and Kryukov were absent. It was a kind of short holiday for the Department. A few worked a little before lunch, but afterwards we all lolled in cafes, and on a couple of occasions even went on a trip to the lake.

At one drinking bout to celebrate an officer's promotion in 1970, Kryukov, as usual, got very drunk and started to look for a fight. This time his victim was Ushakov, the clerk to the Department, a short, weak man who always tried to avoid scandals. Kryukov started to accuse him of something and when the clerk objected, grabbed him by the scruff of the neck and hit him hard against the wall. Ushakov left, but a few minutes later he reappeared in the doorway, a pistol in his hand. "Where's that bloody bastard," he shouted. "I'll kill him to hell." Kryukov reacted quicker than any of us, crying from under the table: "Take the pistol away from that crazy fellow, he will kill me." The pistol was wrested from Ushakov and Kryukov, recovering from his fright, asked to be forgiven. In five minutes they were drinking together to "world peace".

But it was out of character for Kryukov to suffer a defeat like that, and he turned his anger against me and Lavrukhin. He suspected that the pistol affair was our idea. He cursed us and threatened punishment, so that we were soon fed up with him. "You know what," said Lavrukhin, "I've got an idea. Let's put him in a bath filled with cold water, perhaps it will sober him up." We filled the bath, led Kryukov, who could hardly stand, into the bathroom; took all documents and money out of his pockets and then lowered him into the cold water as he was, in uniform, with all his orders and medals. He was so drunk that he hardly reacted. After five minutes, we took him out, put him in a car and told the driver to take him home. Next day Lavrukhin and I waited impatiently to see what Kryukov would do to us. At about ten o'clock he called us in. His first question was: "Where are the documents and the money?" We handed them back to him. He carefully counted the 700 GDR marks, then set about us. "Have you forgotten how to behave towards a senior officer? . . . . . . (unprintable curses). Do you think that you can do what you like at a drinking session? You are mistaken! . . . . . . (unprintable curses)." This went on for 30 to 40 minutes, after which Kryukov calmed down and finally asked us not to tell anyone what had happened. Lavrukhin and I acknowledged our guilt and assured him of secrecy. Thus was unofficial peace declared.

It often happened that the chiefs were to be found drinking hard in one place, in spite of all their differences, while at the same time their subordinates were to be found beating it up in another cafe. At one such gathering, the majority were setting out for home but some of the officers had not had enough, in particular Lieutenant Kemskov and Major Yermakov, who decided to prolong the festivities. Swaying from side to side in a close embrace, they set off in search of a suitable place. It was already late, but they found one cafe where lights still burned and music could be heard, just what the officers needed. But the door was locked. When they hammered at it an attendant explained that there was a private anniversary party in the cafe to which outsiders were not admitted. "Who are you calling outsiders'?" demanded Zemskov who spoke German fluently. "Soviet officers cannot possibly be outsiders and we wish to attend this party." Noticing that both officers could hardly stand, the attendant slammed the door in their faces. Neither Zemskov nor Yermakov liked that. They collected heavy stones and broke all the cafe windows and then, paying not the slightest attention to the panic they had caused, set off home.

Two days later, the German authorities informed Major Tyrin, Bernau Town Commandant, of the unworthy behaviour of certain Soviet officers. Major Tyrin, previously briefed by KGB Major Yermakov, replied that officers could not possibly behave in such a way, and refused to listen to anything further. Thus ended harmlessly, on this particular occasion, a Chekist escapade. But sometimes these drunken brawls got dangerous. There was in our Department a certain Salenkov. He had not been in the KGB long and was by nature a troublemaker and fully conscious of his powers as a KGB worker. At the end of 1972, Salenkov, in civilian clothes, was making merry in one of the cafes of Eberswald and became drunk. When he ordered yet another bottle of vodka, the barmaid refused and asked him to leave. "How dare you contradict me," yelled Salenkov. "I'm a Soviet Chekist and I'll shoot you! " This said, he took out a pistol and aimed at the barmaid. Many people headed for the exit in panic, but the situation was saved by a man who managed to knock the pistol out of Salenkov's hand. A German telephoned the Komendatura and Salenkov was led from the cafe with hands tied. On learning that he was a KGB officer, the Commandant, fearing repercussions, ordered him to be taken home. Subsequently, Salenkov was punished by the head of the Directorate of Special Departments with three days' detention. But in a few weeks all was forgotten and at the beginning of 1973, without serving any extra time, he was promoted lieutenant.

Our Department was not alone in this sort of conduct. Many KGB workers spent and still spend their free time in this way. We frequently heard of top secret orders from Andropov about "exceptionial happenings" within the ranks and about the punishment of those found guilty. As in any other chronicle of crimes, anything at all might turn up: suicides, car accidents with drunken KGB drivers, drunken brawls, shootings on the streets and even crimes. One worker of the Special Department of Ryazan organised a criminal group which concerned itself with the sexual perversion of minors. In 1973, after the militia had unmasked the group, the guilty official was dismissed and the head of the Department concerned, Lieutenant-Colonel Suslov, was reduced to the rank of major. The fact that Suslov's career had come to an end affected him profoundly and he died a week later from a heart attack. It remains a matter for conjecture whether that was suicide or a natural death.

Higher ranks of the KGB behave no better. Once when Kryukov was in a good mood, after drinking in a Bernau cafe, he started to teach me the art of living. "You are still a young officer. There is much you do not know, so listen carefully and learn. To make one's career in the KGB, one needs good connections and graft as well as being able to please one's chiefs. This is very important! The work itself is not so important. If you are not a complete fool, you will always manage to get good results. I myself made one mistake in my life. I was getting on well in KGB headquarters in Moscow. And all because of that bastard General Fedorchuk, I lost everything. At one time, he was here in the GDR as head of the Directorate of Special Departments. I often came here with others from Moscow to check the work of the Special Department. Of course, Fedorchuk did every-thing within his power to please us. Endless drinking bouts; nights out in Berlin with young girls and striptease. Everything we wished. Expensive presents, all paid for officially, of course. In return, we reported to Moscow on the excellently organised work of KGB Special Departments in the GDR.

"In a short while, Fedorchuk was promoted to head of the Third KGB Directorate, and hence my chief. Once, at a party organised by Fedorchuk, I drank a bit too much and told him not to forget that I too had a hand in his career. He did not reply, but some time later I began to feel I had made a blunder. At work, my chiefs started to get at me over trifles. Soon, under some pretext, I was punished and sent to work in the GDR; once there, I was punished again and demoted and that is how I found myself working in this particular Department. Of course, I shall try to get back to Moscow and have already taken steps in that direction, but my career is definitely finished. You must learn from my example. Never speak the truth to one's superiors, look for graft and useful connections instead. Have a good 'sense of smell'. Don't make the same mistakes as one officer who never got beyond lieutenant in 20 years' service. Where he should have licked, he barked, and where he should have barked, he licked. A very dangerous mistake to make! "

Kryukov's story did not reveal much that was new to me—I had already noticed it all during my service—but his words confirmed the tainted nature of the whole system, from top to bottom, in which I served. It is not for nothing that the popular phrase has it that "a fish decays from its head first".

Kryukov did achieve his aim; he was transferred to Moscow as deputy head of the KGB Special Department attached to Special Units of the Moscow Garrison. We travelled together in the same train from Berlin to Moscow, for I was going on leave and he was going to his new post. Before his departure Kryukov got drunk and fought with Boychenko for the last time. He appeared at Berlin's Eastern Station dead drunk. He lolled along the platform dressed in his colonel's uniform; accosted passers-by and before getting into his carriage even urinated in the station dustbin. I took the key from the train attendant and locked him in his compartment to prevent unnecessary incidents.

As well as power over "simple mortals", freedom in personal behaviour and the opportunity to get drunk at official expense, KGB agents have other material privileges. An officer receives three or four times the daily pay of a skilled worker, he also has a splendid flat, the right to buy goods in special shops at reduced prices and much else besides. As for the chiefs, they have absolutely everything they desire.

Even so, it frequently happens that all these privileges are not enough for some. They want still more and often use their official positions for personal gain. This is best demonstrated by examples.

In many ways the USSR is the most powerful military force in the world, spending huge sums on the development of its military-industrial potential, on military science and on supplying armaments to "fraternal socialist countries" and to Third World countries. Indirectly, the USSR participates in many "local" wars (Vietnam, the Middle East and others). All this requires money. Where to get it? The only possibility is at the expense of the people's well-being. Less money is spent on the consumer's needs and on the development of light industry. Some manufactured articles are, therefore, in short supply, such as fridges, furniture, etc, while the quality of others is well below world standards, particularly clothing and footwear.

KGB workers hardly suffer from this at all. Basically, they can either buy anything or "obtain" it, although in the USSR the home-produced goods are of inferior quality to Western products. Consequently KGB officers and civilians serving abroad feverishly buy up all those products. At long last their wishes can be gratified and they forget that Capitalists are supposed to be their worst enemies. East Germany is a kind of showcase of the socialist world, where much emphasis is placed on the population's well-being and on the production of manufactured consumer goods, and it also receives imports from capitalist countries.

The KGB people make full use of their opportunity; they buy furniture, cut-glass, clothing, carpets and footwear: all to be sent home in containers. They are paid higher wages in the GDR, but there is not always enough, or sometimes they simply do not wish to part with it. This is where various "combinations" and "machinations" begin in order to get hold of the desired goods free of charge. The Military Trading Organisation is widely employed to this end. Military Trading (*Voentorg*) shops are officially subordinate to the army. The KGB, having control over all organisations, controls not only the army itself but also these shops.

The head of Military Trading is a Soviet citizen well acquainted with the KGB, and he tries to cultivate a good relationship by rendering its members services at any opportunity. As a rule it works like this: when new supplies are received at Military Trading, the head informs the Department to which he is responsible. KGB officials order goods they want, goods that never find their way into the shops. Subsequently as "old stock" they are reduced in price two or three times below their original value, and are then despatched to the officials' homes straight from store. This is a popular method, used by all KGB agents as well as by Party leaders and army commanders.

But even using this method, the goods have to be paid for, not a lot but still something. Yet it is possible to get them entirely free through undertakings directly subordinated to a KGB Department or to an individual worker. For example, if a worker is "responsible" for food warehouses then the man in charge will supply him with all he needs. Undertakings too are used for gain, whether it be a military radio works or a furniture factory. The director of such a factory will always find it possible to "help" the KGB agent on whom he depends. The agents, in their turn, think about each other's needs. One "obtains" furniture for the others, while another "obtains" spare parts for the car. It is all done under cover; the goods are either written off as "scrap" or are bought for a nominal price.

Not far from Bernau is the "Torpedo" Factory where light vehicles belonging to the Soviet troops in Germany are maintained. My Department was responsible for this factory. Colonel I. T. Shilenko, to whom our Department was subordinated, expressed a wish to "obtain" a Volga car, not buy it. The desire of a chief is law for one of his subordinates. It was decided to make use of the "Torpedo" Factory. One old Volga was designated as useless scrap by the factory and sold to Shilenko for 100 roubles. After purchasing this wreck, Shilenko officially transferred several hundred further roubles to the factory's account. For this money, the factory was to put the car in "decent order". In a few months, in 1970, Shilenko took delivery of the "overhauled" car, which had become a new car, assembled from new parts. The number was the only thing that remained of the old wreck. Shilenko had more than enough money to purchase a car, but who would buy if he can "obtain" it free. In fact, Shilenko never spent a penny unless he had to. He personally telephoned senior Lieutenant Arelanov, who was responsible for the clothes store, and instructed him to obtain several pairs of white underpants and shirts for him. Arelanov promptly complied.

Colonel Shilenko was not an exception: many KGB officers still behave as he did. Colonel Boychenko "obtained" for his wife by the "negative valuation method" several fur coats and "bought" furniture and cut-glass. He also supplied them to his connections. Several times I had to hand over as gifts, the goods he had obtained, dinner services, cut-glass and so forth, when I travelled to Moscow on leave. One gift was to General Soloyev, head of the Special Department of the KGB of the Moscow Okrug anti-aircraft defence force.

At one time in 1972, Major Mikhajlov was head of our KGB Department. He owed his career to his connections with the head of the Personnel Department of the Third KGB Directorate, Major-General Luzhin. Mikhajlov thought neither about work nor Communism: his main preoccupation was personal gain. He "obtained" everything, beginning with furniture, carpets and clothing and ending with a sporting rifle. He did not forget General Luzkin, to whom he regularly sent carpets, dinner services and pornographic literature which could not be obtained in the USSR.

As our Department was responsible for the largest clothing store belonging to the troops in the GDR, we often received orders from the heads of other Special Departments in the GDR for footwear, shirts and uniform trousers. On several occasions, on instructions from the heads of the Department (Boychenko, Strizhenko), I delivered items to the officers stationed in Potsdam; in 1970, to the then deputy head of the KGB Directorate, General Alekseyev, two pairs of shoes and several shirts; or in 1973, to the head of the Personnel Department, Colonel Grigoryev, trousers and shirts. General Titov, at one time head of the KGB Directorate in the GDR, was appointed head of the Special Department for the Leningrad Military District. For his transfer from Potsdam, he was allocated two aircraft, one for himself and his family, the other an AN12 of 30-ton capacity for his household goods. All this was free, of course, the working class take good care of their "servants".

CHAPTER 10

Communism's landed gentry

IN carrying out operational supervision of various units, I had to be permanently in contact with the officers and thus became well acquainted with their daily life, from the lowest ranks to the highest. The whole officer cadre class may be divided into three groups: the High Command of the army; commanders who occupy positions falling within the "nomenclature of the CC of the CPSU", such as divisional commanders, heads of Divisional Political Departments, army commanders, their deputies and above; and officers occupying subordinate positions. The first two groups are members of the "Soviet Mafia".

The High Command, because of its position in the step-shaped structure of society, is directly next to the Politburo and government. Therefore, its members are among those who enjoy great power in the state. Though in the most privileged layer, they are not permitted to enjoy all that the top echelons of the "Mafia", the Politburo and the government, can claim.

Members of the High Command have almost complete power over the whole army and are subordinate only to the Politburo itself and the government, which controls the army in the last resort with the help of the KGB and highly-placed Party officials. As for material privileges, there are practically no limits. Their enormous salaries alone permit them to live better than many Capitalists in the West, but by using their positions and power over the army, they can obtain additional benefits at official expense and are able to arrange luxurious conditions for themselves. They own comfortable villas provided by the army's building battalions at holiday areas, on the Black Sea, on the Baltic coast and in Moldavia. The villas are protected by army detachments, and often the servants in them are soldiers who cost nothing and are highly disciplined. For leave purposes, members of the High Command usually make full use of service aircraft and cars. I would say that the High Command have an even greater degree of security than their "Mafia" colleagues in civilian life: the mass of people they control are in uniform, and are subordinate to military law, which demands immediate obedience. These officers may be compared—with some rare exceptions—with the great landowners of Tsarist Russia during the era of serfdom, who had almost everything they desired and had the right of life or death over their serfs.

Other high-ranking commanders enjoy almost as much power. They can, if need be, make any soldier or extended serviceman appear before a tribunal and be sentenced to several years imprisonment. It does not matter at all whether he is guilty or not; in army conditions, a soldier can always be made to be guilty if need be. Ordinary officers, that is those who do not belong to the so-called "nomenclature ranks", may similarly be brought before a tribunal, if need arises. But more usually, they are simply reprimanded and reduced in rank or given some other form of punishment.

The similarity between highly privileged members of the army and the great landowners is emphasised by the fact that they are both, in a way, owners of tracts of land, lakes and forests. Large expanses of territory in various regions are allocated to the army for training and other purposes. Entire forests and lakes are closed to the civilian population, and the "Soviet Mafia" use these areas for their personal purposes.

Not far from Kaunas in the Lithuanian SSR is a field firing range used for training by one of the airborne divisions. There is a small but beautiful lake, and nearby a villa with its own garden, all permanently guarded by airborne soldiers, not because of the secret experiments carried out there but because the lake is used by their commander, one Army General Margelov, for fishing and hunting. He is well supplied with such lakes and hunting grounds near Kaunas, Tula, Fergana, Pskov and Moldavia. Sometimes he makes use of service aircraft to visit his estates.

Another example shows clearly the pretentious habits of the higher ranking officers. In the summer of 1971, the 20th Guards Army held manoeuvres on GDR territory. The then commander of the Group of Soviet Forces in Germany, Colonel General Kulikov, who is now Army General and Chief of the General Staff, directed the exercise for the most part from his headquarters in Vünsdorf. Kulikov appeared on manoeuvres only once, at the Magdeburg firing range, where he watched the firing practice of the 6th Guards Division. During the previous 24 hours, two engineer battalions spent 20 hours laying a section of asphalt road at considerable cost in money and effort, solely so that he could appear on the range without dirtying his general's uniform. He spent about two hours at the range; crossed the newly-built road only once; watched the firing practice, then departed for Vünsdorf by helicopter. The new road was never used again and it remains a sort of monument to the general. How many such monuments there are on various firing ranges throughout the Soviet Union and the countries of the Warsaw Pact no one can say.

Ordinary members of the "Mafia", the "nomenclature ranks" of the army, are also members of a privileged class who occupy responsible posts and enjoy many advantages beyond the reach of the masses. They are comparatively well-informed about political events, both internally and abroad, as well as about the Politburo's plans for the immediate future. But the fact that they are well-informed by no means signifies that they can influence events, for they are obliged merely to execute decisions taken by the Politburo and government. Information received from the Politburo, the Central Committee of the CPSU and the Political Directorate of the Army is delivered by a secret postal service. Special units exist to store this information, which is closely guarded.

Because it is not easy to keep the masses in subjection, "nomenclature workers" are given privileges which free them from most everyday worries. The posts they occupy carry salaries a great deal higher than those of ordinary officers. They have shops of their own; special departments are equipped for their use in military hospitals; they spend their leave in rest houses closed to other officers. In short, almost everything intended for their use is in some way "special". Even visits to theatres and cinemas are free, and they get the best seats.

In spite of all their privileges, some of them want still more. They use every means at their disposal for personal gain, the state purse, their official position and power over subordinates. In 1970, the commander of Rear Supply Services of the 20th Guards Army, Deputy Army Commander Major-General Zhirnov, made use of his position as quartermaster to order *Voentorg* shops to sell meat and other products intended for consumption by the troops. The money flowed into his pocket. The fact that the portions served to the troops in some units became smaller was nobody's business. This situation continued for about a year, until one of the saleswomen in the shop threatened, after a quarrel with her superiors, to make the facts known. Frightened by the prospect of publicity, General Zhirnov stopped the sale of army food. The saleswoman was subsequently "discovered" in some kind of theft; it was all prearranged and she was put behind bars for two years.

In the 20th Guards Army, the name of Lieutenant-General Sivenok became a synonym for extreme greed. He was loath to spend a half-penny of his salary if he could avoid it. Everything, furniture, carpets, dinner services and pictures, were officially purchased for his office or for the officers' quarters, but in reality they were sent off to his own house. He ate and drank in the officers' mess—free of course—and sometimes even at the expense of mess personnel.

These examples are not exceptions; they are daily occurrences and no one would even notice such behaviour on the part of "real

Communists". Sometimes "nomenclature workers" go too far, with unpleasant results. This happened when one of them got too well-known among the public because of his shady dealings and cast a stain on the "clean face" of the Party. Major-General Pitkevich, a brigade commander in East Berlin and head of the Berlin Garrison, had connections—or "blat" as it is known—in the Ministry of Defence of the USSR. For this reason, he felt secure and excelled in his shameless passion for money. He established a criminal link with a serviceman in charge of the food stores. At his request, the soldier who had served about 15 years in the GDR and had many German connections, began to sell products cheaply to the public. Later he implicated in the illegal traffic a number of his friends in charge of various other stores. Things went well and General Pitkevich pocketed tens of thousands of marks. But soon many of those serving in the brigade learned of his earnings on the side. All manner of tales got about, and some army men referred to him as a twister and a scoundrel. It is forbidden to even think harshly of the "Mafia", let alone speak harshly. The KGB intervened and upon its recommenda-tion, the Military Procurator started investigations. The inquiries naturally did not result in the general being blamed. He was just a trusting individual and that corrupt serviceman had exploited and abused his trust. Furthermore, the general had never pocketed any money! The serviceman was sentenced to one and a half years depri-vation of liberty by a military tribunal. However, too many people knew about the general; he was transferred to the USSR, and soon afterwards was retired on a pension.

These ordinary members of the "Mafia" behave no better in their private lives either. There are times when they behave like the worst drunkards. In November 1973, the commander of the 6th Guards Division, Colonel [now General] Sotskov and the Head of the Political Department of that same Division, Colonel Chelyshev, celebrated October Revolution Day too well. They went for a stroll round Bernau with their wives. The fresh air apparently had a beneficial effect and both men decided to go into a cafe for a glass of vodka. As usual, the second glass followed and then the third and soon the two were drunk again. It was already late and they started to go home without paying, but the cafe owner locked the door and demanded the money. Sotskov and Chelyshev, and their wives, started to shout that they had already paid and accused the owner of being a crook. The owner telephoned the police and Komendatura and reported the unseemly behaviour of the two officers, but he did not know that one of them was Head of the Bernau Garrison, and the other his deputy for political matters, or that the local authorities were to some extent dependent on them. It is easy to imagine the

predicament of Major Tyrin, the Komendant, and of the police chief
when they arrived. Neither knew what to do, but Colonel Sotskov
saved the day. He ordered Major Tyrin to sort out this "scoundrel
and twister", and then with Chelyshev and their wives, went off home
in the Komendant's car.

Major Tyrin paid the cafe owner for the vodka and the police chief
ordered him to keep his mouth shut. The incident was forgotten by
everyone except Major Tyrin, who promptly telephoned us at the
KGB Department. Naturally, our Department took no action, but
"just in case" a note was made in the relevant documents. Who
knows? Everything may come in handy some day! The vast majority
of officers, platoon commanders, company commanders, battalion
commanders, regimental commanders and many others, do not belong
to "nomenclature workers". These ordinary officers are from all
sections of society, workers, peasants, intelligentsia, Party members
and so forth. Any young man under 21 with a high-school education
who has been politically checked may enter an Officers' Military
School. The length of study differs and may last from three to six
years. The cadets are subjected to intensive training and are indoctrinated to become convinced Communists. They are taught that the
fact of their belonging to the officers corps is evidence of the special
trust placed in them, and they must be especially proud of their gold
shoulder straps and stars. Infusion of Communist ideas does not end
with graduation from military school; indeed it is increased still
further and is continued right up to the time of retirement. The aim
of all this ideological training is the creation of a reliable officer
corps devoted to the régime.

Under the Soviet system, an ordinary officer occupies a higher
place than, let us say, engineers or technicians or sections of the
bureaucracy. He gets higher pay and more security, but there the
advantages end. Like other Soviet citizens, or even more so, he must
obey laws strictly and fulfil any instructions of the Politburo and
government. In exchange for small privileges, he must always be
ready, on orders "from above", to stand in defence of the régime
against its "external" and, if need arises, also "internal" enemies.
This happens at times of disturbances(!) among the workers which
still occur in spite of all the efforts made in the USSR and in
"fraternal socialist states". The most vivid examples showing how
the "glorious Soviet Army" executes the orders of the leadership
were the suppression of the workers in Hungary, the GDR and
Czechoslovakia.

How do these officers live? What interests them and how do they
spend their free time? The 16th Motorised Rifle Regiment of the
6th Guard Motorised Rifle Division stationed in the GDR in Bad-

Freienwald provided one example. A Motorised Rifle Regiment is a separate, independent unit, having also tank, artillery, anti-aircraft and other detachments. In all, there are 180 officers in the regiment, with 1,800 men. None of the officers from the commanding officer to platoon commander, is a "nomenclature worker" and, therefore, the regiment is not among the privileged ones. But there is still no equality among the officers: they create their own subdivisions. This discrimination shows not only in different duties, rights and pay, but also in their personal lives, their behaviour and relations with each other.

Some, like the regimental commander, his five deputies and the secretary of the regimental Party Committee, are privileged and form a so-called "regimental élite". They play an important role in the unit's life, while attempting to gain everything possible out of their positions, even though they do not enjoy the same possibilities as the select few like "nomenclature workers" or KGB men. The first thing they exploit is the *Voentorg* shop set up for officers and the extended servicemen. The trafficking I described earlier does not occur here. The élite cannot enjoy this facility, but nevertheless they are still able to extract some benefit.

Goods coming up for sale in *Voentorg* shops are divided into those in short supply and ordinary goods. To distribute the scarce goods such as dinner services, carpets and furniture fairly, a "shop commission" is elected at a general meeting of officers' wives. The commission usually consists of three to five women who make lists of the officers' names, listing the goods in short supply bought by officers' families punctiliously. These lists are compiled over the years and decide the turn of each family. Officially the regimental commander and his deputies must in theory keep strictly in their turn. In practice, when each lot of new supplies is received, the wives of the regimental commander and his deputies go to the *Voentorg* shop an hour before it opens; choose whatever takes their fancy; pay on the spot and take it home. Everyone knows about it, but most people prefer to stay silent.

Such incidents also happened in the 16th Regiment; the cause of it all was the wife of the regimental commander, Lieutenant-Colonel Morozov. Not only did she frequently buy goods in short supply out of turn but also boasted about her purchases to other wives, which made them jealous. In 1973, it was the turn of the wife of the senior regimental doctor, senior Lieutenant Vizner, to buy a dinner service, but it had been carried off by Mrs Morozova. Mrs Vizner set out to "clarify the situation". Mrs Vizner demanded that Mrs Morozova should return the dinner service to the shop immediately and when Mrs Morozova refused, a fight ensued with the women slapping and pulling each other's hair. Mrs Morozova's husband found a pretext to retaliate on Vizner himself and wrote a bad report, which resulted in his being transferred to the USSR to serve in a provincial military district.

When in October 1973, the wives held their general meeting to elect a new "shop commission" for 1974, senior Lieutenant Anisimov's wife proposed that in future the regimental commander and his deputies should take their turn with the others in buying goods in short supply. Mrs Morozova jumped up and shouted to her husband, who was chairing the meeting with his deputy: "You are the regimental commander, make her shut up! Stop her gob!" Colonel Morozov, with a gesture cut short Mrs Anisimova's speech and announced: "All of us here abroad want to buy as many rags as we can. So do I. I am the regimental commander. I've always taken things out of turn and shall continue to do so. The same applies to my deputies. And you will get what is left over." He kept his word and things continued in the same way.

Although the pay of the commander and his deputies was considerable, they resorted to obtaining money "on the side" to get the quantities of goods they wanted. They took meat, butter, flour, bread and other products from regimental stores without payment, and all kinds of deals were arranged with East Germans.

From 1969 to 1972, Malofeyev, deputy commander of the regiment, with the approval of his commanding officer, allowed a German collective farmer of the Bad-Freienwald region to graze his sheep on the firing range, and in return received 20,000 marks which were divided equally between the commander and his deputies. Malofeyev also sold butter and meat from regimental stores to the East Germans. When he retired in 1972, he left for Odessa, but not before he had despatched four container loads of carpets, furniture and cut crystal.

His replacement, Lieutenant-Colonel Tertyshnyj, decided to organise his additional income differently, that is, not to steal but to "earn" it. He signed a contract with the laundry and bath combine in Bad-Freienwald. About a hundred soldiers from the 16th Regiment daily worked at this combine for three months and their earnings went to Tertyshnyj and his deputies. Major Konik, deputy regimental Political Chief, and another deputy regimental commander, Lieutenant-Colonel Tsetskhladze, concluded similar profitable agreements with collective farms.

The "earnings" method is popular. Wherever Soviet units are stationed in the GDR, soldiers work at German undertakings situated near garrisons. They operate wherever unskilled workers are needed: they dig foundations for new buildings; collect rubbish from building sites, and clean out pigstyes. It does not matter that the work is dirty—

it helps their "motherland commanders" to have a good life, although a decree of the Minister of Defence forbids the employment of Soviet servicemen in German undertakings. Such work is, therefore, always organised and carried out under the guise of "international assistance", with the aim of improving friendship between German and Soviet citizens. Occasionally these schemes are genuine, such as joint efforts to build "houses of friendship" or equip pioneer camps, and they are widely publicised in newspapers and the radio. But events like these are rare. About 98 per cent of servicemen working in German undertakings earn money that goes straight into the pockets of their commanding officers.

The higher authorities are well aware of what goes on but prefer not to notice it officially. Their attitude is that although not members of the "Mafia" élite, the officers are responsible specialists, and, if they can extract some benefit from their official position which enables them to live better than the others, that makes them satisfied, and so more devoted to the Soviet régime. The fact that they are a bit crooked can be forgiven. What will one not forgive a devoted and obedient servant in order to have peace and order in one's house?

After the successful completion of deals "on the side", the regimental commander and his deputies together with all their wives were in the habit of holding drinking sessions. Drink was paid for by the soldiers' earnings and the hors d'oeuvres were prepared from supplies taken from regimental stores. As a rule the sessions were wild; vodka flowed like a river. These all-night celebrations were often attended by East Germans, the representatives of Bad-Freienwald authorities and directors of undertakings, where the soldiers worked. When everyone was drunk the party became an orgy. On one occasion the wives made Colonel Murashchenko undress completely and stand in the middle of the room while they danced round him. "International friendships" took an unorthodox turn. It sometimes happened that the wife of the regimental commander, Mrs Morozova, spent the night with Lieutenant-Colonel Shemerling, of the National People's Army of the GDR, while his own wife was sleeping with Colonel Murashchenko. Usually everyone knew all about it, except those most closely concerned.

And that is how the "regimental élite" lives. The other officers live in hope of better days. Some try to "organise" something for themselves, but the possibilities are limited and most such attempts end unpleasantly. So in the summer of 1973, the wife of senior Lieutenant Semenov was caught red-handed trying to steal an expensive dress from a German shop and was arrested by the German police, who handed her over to the Soviet authorities. Mrs Semenova was warned about her behaviour being unfitting to a Soviet citizen and sent home to her husband. Here the incident ended. It did not cause much commotion, as it was considered quite usual. There are still officers who think deeply about all that happens in the Soviet Army and in the USSR itself, but there are very few and against them stands the KGB. Such people are dangerous, for they think too much!

CHAPTER 11

Rank-and-file privations

M Y activities were concerned not only with Soviet officers and East Germans, but also with rank-and-file soldiers. Living conditions for these men of the Group of Soviet Forces in Germany are even more severe than in the military districts on Soviet territory. The two years which a soldier serves in Germany are years of privation and torment, and they can only be compared to a term of imprisonment.

He spends these years in barracks, on the training ground or on the firing range. It is strictly forbidden to leave the encampment. He never gets outside leave, even on Saturday or Sunday or on any holiday. Only occasionally, a few soldiers in the charge of an officer visit a German town or village where they are stationed. Such excursions are rare and only the best and most disciplined soldiers can go.

The barracks themselves are mostly old buildings used by Hitler's Wehrmacht. The only thing that has changed is the number of people who occupy them. Where formerly a German company was quartered now a whole battalion lives there, and where a German battalion lived, a regiment has to be accommodated. Thus the Bad-Freienwald barracks, which at one time housed a motor-cycle battalion, now houses the 16th Motorised Rifle Regiment (2,000 men) and a rocket unit. The walls and roof of the building are original but inside everything has been rearranged. All the partitions that subdivided the barracks into small bedrooms have been removed and large areas have been created to hold 100 men. The attics have been converted into living space. All cupboards and other "unnecessary" things, which somehow softened the severity of the soldier's life, have been thrown out. A Soviet soldier does not need such things, for he lives a spartan existence. He folds his uniform each night and puts it on a stool; his overcoat hangs in the corridor and his dress uniform is kept in store. Why should a soldier need a cupboard, if he has nothing to keep in it? It is this rationing of space which permits the housing of 500 men where formerly there were 150 to 200 German soldiers. "Cramped but not offended" as the Russian proverb goes.

What it is like during the night in quarters where 100 people are sleeping cramped together can be imagined. I happened a couple of times to be in these sleeping quarters at night. They literally stink and the first moments seem unbearable, for one wants to rush out immediately. Only after 10 or 15 minutes does one become slightly accustomed to it. To leave the barracks and go into the street is simply to feel drunk with the fresh air. One can only feel astonished how anyone could sleep under such conditions. Washing facilities are no better. In the basement of the barracks are the shower rooms, each with two or three showers. According to established practice, the soldiers have to wash once a week, usually on Saturdays. The whole regiment has to get washed in four or five hours, and that when there is only one room with three showers per battalion, and the Motorised Rifle battalion consists of over 400 men. The battalion gets washed a company at a time, each being allowed an hour.

Eating arrangements, or as they are called in military parlance, "receipt of food", are also interesting. Each unit has its own dining-room built to feed all the men at one sitting. In the 16th Regiment such a dining-room holds 2,000 men. Large tables with benches attached are set out, each table seating 10 to 15 men. Just before dinner, a pile of metal plates is placed on the table together with two containers of food. One holds the first course, soup, and the second holds kasha, or meat and potatoes or fish and potatoes. The soldiers march to the dining-room singing. Each man takes his appointed place. When all are seated, one soldier at each table serves out the food to his comrades and the meal begins.

The scene as 2,000 men try to eat is unimaginable. There is the cramped space, noise, and shouts, as someone has lost his portion, someone has lost his spoon, or someone's meat has been stolen. Again, as in the sleeping quarters, the air is thick, especially in the summer. The smell of food mixes with the odour of sweating bodies and the temperature is only a little lower than in a Turkish bath. They are given only 30 minutes to eat after which, at a command, they march back to barracks. Such eating arrangements are customary throughout the army.

Barracks are equipped with loudspeakers which transmit Moscow Radio's programme No 1, or the programme of the Group of Soviet Forces in Germany, Volga Radio. The men are permitted to own their own radios, but with certain limitations: they are kept in the company storeroom and are issued only on Sundays and holidays. This limitation was introduced on the initiative of the political workers who feared that the men would otherwise listen to transmissions from Radio Free Europe, BBC and Voice of America.

The soldier's day is so planned that he is always occupied: drill, political indoctrination, training and cleaning weapons. Before going to bed, he has one hour of free time, in which he must prepare for the next day; clean his uniform; sew on a new collar and, if there is time, write a letter home. At weekends, he stays in barracks, but sports days are arranged instead of the usual training. These usually begin with a cross-country race of three to five kilometres and afterwards the men march to the regimental stadium to watch sporting competitions.

Monthly pay is 15 marks. With this the soldier must buy all the toilet articles he needs, envelopes and paper. Cigarettes are issued free—but what cigarettes—filled with dirty tobacco with no filters! Soldiers call them "contraceptives" or "TB" and joke about winning a war against America by merely handing out these cigarettes to the other side. To supplement their meagre pay, the men sell to the East Germans cheaply such things as watches brought from home, radios or cans of stolen petrol. As they are not allowed outside the encampment, the sales entail great risks. They have to be carefully prepared and usually only old hands take part. One or more pretend to fall sick and are excused training by the doctor. They can then take their "stock" from hiding places; climb over the fence and try to find a buyer, sometimes offering the goods at the roadside to German motorists. It is all very cheap, for a good watch or radio costs 30 to 50 marks; 20 litres of petrol plus the can cost 20 marks (a litre in the GDR costs 150 marks). If the soldiers fall into the hands of a patrol, their profits are confiscated and they are sent to the guard house for a week or two.

Despite the severity of service, it would all be bearable if the position of the soldiers was not affected by a fundamental discrimination between different groups, based on length of service, with one group persecuting another. According to the Constitution, every male Soviet citizen of 18 years is liable for military service for two years. The call-ups take place twice a year, in spring and autumn, while at the same time demobilisation is carried out of men who have served their time. Therefore, there are four call-up groups in the Soviet army at any given time. There are those who have only started their service, those who are ending their first year, those who have started their second year of service and finally those who are serving out the last six months, crossing off each passing day on the calendar. Officially, all call-up groups are considered equal and no long-service soldier has any advantages over a young soldier. But in practice, the mass of soldiers, isolated in barracks from the outside world, live according to their own special laws.

The almost complete isolation and the strict discipline take all meaning from such concepts as independence, individuality and personal freedom, let alone alcohol and girls. They simply do not exist. As a result, other values come into play. For example, a soldier wants to have a good place in the barracks so that his bed stands near the window where he can get enough fresh air at night. He does not want to wear an old uniform or torn boots. He wants to be given the largest piece of meat when the food is divided out and he does not want to do dirty work like cleaning lavatories and collecting rubbish. But in accordance with the unwritten laws of service life, all the advantages go to the long-service men. Young soldiers feel it from the first day: their new uniforms pass to the old soldiers and in exchange they are given worn boots, worn belt, an overcoat with holes burnt in it. Next, the old soldiers start to "teach" the young ones the military rules. *Salagi*[1]—as raw recruits are called—are compelled to clean the old soldiers' boots; wash their uniforms, and clean the barracks and lavatories.

In the dining-room, where old soldiers and *Salagi* sit at the same table, strict discipline reigns. One of the youngsters, appointed by the old soldiers, serves the food. "You, *Salaga,* must dish out the food as it is done in good families, according to merit!" one of the old men tells him first. Long-service men are served first, and of course with the best pieces of meat and fish, while the young soldiers get whatever is left over. At lunch or dinner when butter is issued, it goes mainly to the long-service men, who claim that butter is bad for the *Salagi* as it might cause unnecessary fat, which is a hindrance in doing one's duty. *Salagi* may not start to eat before the old soldiers. They may not talk during the meal as that is the old men's privilege. They must not be greedy and must give the best pieces to a senior colleague. As for butter, the youngsters are advised to put their minute portion on the corner of a slice of bread and to eat towards the butter, meanwhile keeping their eye on it. This, says the old soldier, makes one feel that the whole slice is covered in butter, and the recruits keep strictly to this ruling.

The youngsters' pay is also raided. On receiving their miserable 15 marks, they have to give five to aid the old men, who also use shoe polish and other items bought with the remaining ten marks. Each evening after lights out in the barracks, the following ritual is observed: a young soldier stands in the middle of the dormitory and announces in a loud voice "Attention, attention! Listen everybody! Our revered old men have 51 days 20 hours and 30 minutes left until their demobilisation. Good night, old men!"

If a young soldier infringes one of these unwritten laws or in the opinion of the long-servicemen simply does not show the respect due, he has to face a "military tribunal", with one old soldier playing the part of judge, another the defence counsel and a third the procurator. All the young ones have to attend. The *Salaga* usually pleads guilty

---

[1] Translator's note: *Salaga* is a fish found in the Neva River.

and the tribunal decides on how many "hot" or "cold" he is to be given. "Hot" means so many blows with a spoon on bare bottom. "Cold" means the same thing but with trousers still on. If it is 15 "hot", the victim lies on his bed and a *young* soldier—it must be one of the young ones, to emphasise the moral humiliation—sits on top of him and beats his backside with a spoon. Usually, after such punishment, the victim cannot sit properly for a week.

These practices are prohibited, but although the officers know what goes on they take no action. They consider that relations between old soldiers and new recruits strengthen general discipline. In theory, any young soldier can complain to an officer about injustices, but it rarely happens. The officer goes home at the end of the day after punishing an old soldier, but the soldiers will be left together in the barracks, and then the hour of retribution comes. They arrange a "dark" night for anyone who has complained. They cover his head with a blanket and start to beat him. They beat cruelly and mercilessly. After such a thrashing, the soldier usually lands in hospital for a couple of days. It is practically impossible to find the perpetrators. These floggings have been known to result in death. In the summer of 1973, old soldiers serving in stores belonging to the 20th Guards Army so beat a young soldier called Ivanchenko that he died the next morning.

Not only do the common soldiers have to endure individual tortures, they are also subject to suffering imposed *en masse* by the authorities. Some years ago an atomic test explosion took place somewhere East of Lake Baikal. During, or shortly after the test, a motorised rifle regiment of the Soviet Army was ordered to drive through the radioactive area. The troops were told beforehand that there was no danger.

After the exercise, it was found that 70 per cent of the unit had been seriously affected by the radiation and required hospital treatment. All these soldiers were taken to a military hospital in Moscow for persons exposed to radiation and I was told by a Soviet Army lieutenant-colonel, who had been in the same hospital, that in 1973 they were still treating these poor bastards, who had been use as guinea-pigs.

Some young soldiers cannot stand the hellish conditions of service and commit suicide. In the 20th Guards Army alone, according to secret statistics, suicides among young soldiers numbered 16 in 1971, 24 in 1972 and 33 in 1973. The figures speak for themselves.

In September 1971, one of my informers who was reporting on whether any servicemen was thinking of deserting to the West or had made any anti-Soviet remarks, said he had found a notebook belonging to a soldier called Marushchenko in which he wrote of his intention to commit suicide. I telephoned the deputy Political Officer of the 16th Motorised Rifle Regiment, Lieutenant-Colonel Pustovoy, to warn him and advised him to take measures to prevent the suicide. He told me that he knew Marushchenko, whom he considered abnormal, so there was no question of any suicide. I did not believe him, and although it was no affair of mine since the KGB has no interest in suicides, I decided to summon Marushchenko to my office. He turned out to be a small, sickly individual. He looked frightened and it took some time before he "melted" and started to talk.

Before call-up, he had married and a pregnant wife was waiting for him. As a civilian, he had heard a lot of propaganda stressing the good points of army life and he became convinced of its justice, but the reality was different. He told me how the old soldiers tormented the recruits. It appeared that Marushchenko had twice complained to the deputy Political Officer and had been beaten cruelly on both occasions by the long-service men. He ended with the words: "I think, comrade Senior Lieutenant, that such things only happen in our regiment. Nobody believes me, neither the commanding officer nor the deputy Political Officer." I could not tell him that similar things happen throughout the army but offered to help him.

"I do not trust anyone any more," he answered. "You see, no one trusts me, they all think I am abnormal."

Trying to comfort him, I said that if things were bad he could come to my office at any time and I would try to help. And with that, we parted. Three days later I was awakened at night by a telephone call. Colonel Pustovos, the deputy regimental Political Officer, was on the line: "Two hours ago Marushchenko shot himself. In his pocket they found a letter addressed to you." I said that no one was to touch the letter and in 15 minutes I was there. Maruschenko lay on his back on the ground; there were three bullet holes in his chest, the automatic rifle lay beside him.

"The lad died in vain," I thought. "He could have lived—and a pregnant wife waited for him at home." I took the envelope which somebody held out to me. On the envelope was "To that rather special Senior Lieutenant"—Mauruschenko did not know my name. Back in my office, I read it.

"Comrade Senior Lieutenant, I can stand it no longer. All round me are untruths. The humiliations continue. The officers do not wish to know about it. I ask you to see that all is put right in the regiment. No one believes what I say. I give my life to confirm my words."

"Poor Marushchenko," I sat thinking, "you died like a hero and all in vain! No one will even remember you, except your relations and your wife." And in fact, the soldiers of the 16th Regiment were told that he was mentally abnormal, and the incident was forgotten in a couple of weeks.

In the summer of 1973, in the same 16th Regiment, a young soldier named Dzhavadze tried to commit suicide. A Georgian by nationality, he spoke Russian badly, which led to unending jokes by his comrades and many humiliations at the hands of the old soldiers. Even the officers often called him *Churka* (a form of insult). Once, unable to bear it, Dzhavadze went to the mirror, took a cut-throat razor and cut his throat. An ambulance was called and his life was saved, but he remained an invalid for the rest of his life. In his farewell letter, he had asked that his relations should be told that he had been wounded in an accident.

Not all soldiers resignedly endure the inhuman army life or commit suicide. Some express their protests in another way: they desert, usually taking a weapon with them. In most cases such desertions are spontaneous; human patience is simply exhausted. It usually happens when the *Salaga* is put on guard duty at a favourable spot, with an automatic rifle and ammunition. Left alone as time drags, the youngster recalls all the insults, and decides then and there to end it all and deserts. The army and KGB, with the assistance of MfS and GDR police, launch a search. Sometimes an entire division takes part, whole regions are surrounded, armed posts are set up on roads and railway stations. The population is warned of the danger from an armed attacker. The operation begins to look like a war against partisans, or, to compare it with the West, like a fight against terrorists.

In the summer of 1970, Private Dzyuban deserted from the 16th Regiment taking an automatic rifle and 60 cartridges. About 5,000 soldiers in armoured vehicles were deployed in the search, together with the GDR police of Bad-Freienwald, Eberwald and Bernaud. The hunt lasted eight days, during which Dzyuban robbed two cafes and terrorised the population. On the ninth day he was found in a wood near Bad-Freienwald. A battalion surrounded him and, after several warning bursts from a machine-gun, he surrendered. He was sentenced by a military tribunal to two years in a "disciplinary battalion".

In 1969, a tragedy occurred in an isolated radio company stationed near Eyzenakh in the GDR. The commander was a cruel man and a drunkard. Conditions in the company were inhuman: soldiers were punished for the slightest mistakes. Everyone suffered, young and old. This time, it was one of the old soldiers, Private Ivanov, who snapped. Once the platoon in which he served was detailed to guard a military target. Ivanov had only just been relieved and with the thought of a rest, was opening the neck of his tunic. The platoon commander promptly sentenced him for being improperly dressed. Then the lieutenant went into the tent where several privates and sergeants were waiting for him to talk to them. Ivanov, who was a constant butt of the lieutenant's complaints, took an automatic; followed the officer into the tent; fired a number of rounds; then rushed out of the tent; threw the automatic into the bushes and disappeared into the forest. The shots killed the lieutenant and two sergeants, and three soldiers were seriously wounded. Some hours later, Ivanov was arrested. During the investigation, it was established that he was frequently unjustly punished. About two months before this incident, he had attempted suicide. With his last, but far from first punishment, the lieutenant had signed his own death warrant. Ivanov was executed by firing squad at the beginning of 1970.

In 1973, I took part in the search for a young soldier named Yashkin belonging to the 81st Motorised Rifle Regiment stationed in Eberwald. The reasons for his desertion were the same, humiliations imposed by old soldiers and numerous punishments. Although about 7,000 soldiers and the whole police force of the Bad-Freienwald region were thrown into the search for him, he managed to stay free for 14 days. He stole two cars, eventually crashing them, and looted four cafes. Yashkin moved about at night and avoided all control posts on roads, while during the day he slept in the woods. For three days, he hid in a shed of a house on the outskirts of a village belonging to a newly-married young couple. At night he slept buried deep in straw and during the day, after the owners had left, he stole their food. But on the third day, the young wife returned home unexpectedly. When he demanded money, the terrified woman gave him 70 marks, but he raped her and stole her watch before running into the woods. Soviet patrols and German police with a dog were sent out and in a couple of hours Yashkin was captured. He was sentenced to three years in a forced labour camp.

Private Korneyev deserted in December 1973 after only two months in the same regiment. He evaded capture until the fourth night when, suffering from hunger, he broke into the house of an old German woman who had a grown-up daughter visiting her. Armed with a metal bar, Korneyev looked for the kitchen; stumbled and awakened the occupants. When the old woman screamed, he struck her on the head with the bar, but the daughter jumped out of a window and raised the alarm. Shaken by what had happened, Korneyev stayed in the house, awaiting the arrival of the Soviet patrols and the police and there he was arrested. The old woman died a few hours later.

These are not isolated incidents; in fact they are a regular occurrence among troops in Germany. Soldiers frequently desert during the summer as they can sleep outdoors then and food is not such a problem. Up to 12 or 14 soldiers have deserted at one time in the summer months, and many of these desertions end in crime, robbery, rape and murder. Deserters have made off not only with automatic rifles but armoured cars and even tanks. In 1971, in one of the tank regiments of the 8th Guards Army, a young soldier, desperate over treatment by his officers, decided to avenge himself in his own way.

He got into a tank, drove up to regimental headquarters, trained the tank's gun onto the headquarters and fired, but he was in such a nervous state that the shell whistled over the rooftop and landed on a German house. He turned the tank round; broke through the boundary fence and drove along the road towards the village. A platoon of soldiers in armoured vehicles was sent after him. The tank's engine stalled not far from the village, but the soldier stayed in it and was quickly surrounded by curious boys. The armoured vehicles soon arrived at the spot. The soldier opened the tank's hatch and started to toss out hand grenades. Several boys were killed when the first grenade exploded, and the vehicles withdrew a short distance. The soldier continued to toss out grenades until one of them struck the tank's hatch; fell back inside the tank and killed him.

Officially, the GDR is an independent state and, according to the law, Soviet soldiers who commit crimes against GDR citizens should be judged by GDR courts. But, up to the present, not a single Soviet soldier has answered for his crime before a German court. The German authorities' role is merely to ensure that GDR citizens know as little as possible of the crimes committed by Soviet soldiers, and also to ensure that those who do know keep their mouths shut. Unnecessary chatter from them could cast a shadow on the Soviet Union, which is held up as an ideal for GDR Communists to follow.

Bearing in mind the living conditions of the troops, they might be expected to become unreliable and refuse to carry out orders at crucial moments, but, remarkable as it may seem, this is *not* the case.

Firstly, the Soviet Army possesses a huge politico-propaganda apparatus equipped with the latest information techniques. It is permanently impressed upon the soldier that all the difficulties he suffers, are the fault of the Capitalist countries, who are prepared to launch a new war. He is imbued with a hatred for the Capitalist world and for other enemies of Socialism and Communism. The so-called "World Gendarme", the United States of America, and its "bandit army" comes in for particularly fierce attack. There are posters hanging in the barracks showing pictures of American soldiers killing women, children and old people in Vietnam. The West German

Bundeswehr is characterised as an Army of Revenge, created on the fascist model, the majority of whose high command and part of its officer corps are made up of former Nazis. NATO soldiers are also generally portrayed as bandits and murderers. And all this is daily and persistently knocked into the heads of youths of 18 to 20.

Secondly, inhuman living conditions keep the soldiers tensed like a compressed spring. Daily drilling, shouting and punishment make them aggressive. They dream only of the day when they can leave the hated barrack walls, if only for a short time. They get the opportunity during exercises; there is no need then for drilling, no need for cleaning out hated toilets and all are equal, both young and old servicemen. They enjoy expeditions even more, as it was during the occupation of Czechoslovakia. They can give vent to aggressive feelings against their enemies, the real cause of all their misfortunes. It matters little who those enemies are, Czechs, Germans, Poles or Americans. Soviet soldiers fulfil their patriotic and international duty.

CHAPTER 12

Time for decision

THE time has now come to return to my personal narrative and to answer the question: why did I become hostile to the Soviet régime? The original reasons for this were my political and, to put it simply, human convictions which were fundamentally at variance with the ideology of the present régime in the Soviet Union. I was not able to come to terms with the Soviet system of inherent violence and inhuman oppression, with the repression and persecution of everyone displeasing to the régime, with the absence of democratic freedoms, with the unscrupulous exploitation of the workers for the good of those in authority, with the all-pervasive ideological conditioning directed towards completely fooling Soviet citizens and with the many other injustices with which Soviet society abounds.

Behind this short answer lie long years of meditation and doubt. I have already said that it began while I was still at school, when small and at first glance seemingly insignificant negative manifestations in Soviet society began imperceptively to undermine my faith in Communism: "the bright future of man". I witnessed many of the injustices of the Soviet régime at first hand in the officers' school and in the army. My work in the KGB played a decisive role. Only then did I really understand what Communism was, and saw the complete cynicism of the Soviet system with my own eyes. I personally had to take part in such measures—or, as the KGB calls them, "operations" —when criminals were created out of innocent people and heroes and idols out of scoundrels; when literally on account of a couple of justifiable criticisms about the Soviet leadership people were sent to prisons, to labour camps and to mental institutions.

Gradually and steadily there ripened within me a protest against all this. I came to understand that it was not certain individuals, like Stalin, Beria, Andropov, Brezhnev, who were to blame for the crimes committed in the Soviet Union, but the whole inhuman system, the whole Soviet régime.

My "awakening" was a long and painful process. At one stage, during the first two years of my employment in the KGB, I felt that I did not want to recognise this. "What do you need?" I asked myself. "You are numbered among the élite, the 'chosen', you have something which many others do not have. What are others to you?

Life is full of injustice anyway and you can't change it." I tried
to buy off my conscience; the more so because a promising career
lay ahead of me. Despite my youth I was achieving success in my
work, for which I had received recognition from my superiors and
had gained promotion. I had already become a captain at the age of
27. Maybe I would have remained and continued working for the
KGB if I had only been concerned with counter-intelligence and if
I had not carried out persecutions against Soviet citizens who opposed
the injustices of the régime. I probably would have tried to adjust
myself somehow to Soviet authority and to keep out of the struggle
for justice. However, counter-intelligence duties in the KGB also
include secret police functions. So both the struggle for justice and
injustice often came within the scope of my activity and of my
official responsibilities. Furthermore, in the course of my official duty,
I had to defend injustice and suppress justice, to deal with those
who defended justice. This situation did not allow the conflict inside
me, the struggle with my own conscience, to abate.

Sometimes I despised myself: "Foul police agent," I would think
at such times, "your privileges, authority and material well-being are
ill-gotten, at the expense of innocent victims with whose persecution
you are involved. They have enough courage to fight. But you? You
repress them—hangman! Coward! "

Of course, it was impossible to endure such an inner struggle.
Sooner or later I would have to come to a decision, for the régime
or against it. This happened in 1972 when I finally decided to make
the break, indeed not only to break with the régime but to join the
struggle against it.

It is, of course, easy to say "I have decided to fight against the
Soviet régime", but how would this look in reality? What would I
have to do? Could I create an underground anti-Soviet organisation?
For me, an official in the KGB, there was no possibility of doing this.
In my position the risk was very great, and who would believe that
I was not an agent provocateur?

So, for me, there existed only one real possibility where, with the
use of my knowledge and qualifications, I could inflict a great deal
of harm on the Soviet régime: to establish links with one of the
Western intelligence services. Someone reading these words might say
they are akin to treason. But I did not betray my country. I betrayed
a régime which has oppressed and is oppressing my country. I no
longer wish to serve the régime which acts in a merciless fashion
internally against the workers and is dangerous and aggressive in its
external policy to the outside world. The USSR contains within itself
a threat not only to the peoples of the Soviet Union but also to the
majority of countries of the world. To defend such a régime is

treachery, to fight it, no.

My decision endangered my life. At the first mistake, I would be arrested and almost certainly shot. Such a mistake could be made while establishing the very first contact with Western intelligence. But, above all, how to establish this contact? It was very complicated even in my position where I myself, as a member of Soviet counter-intelligence, was directly involved in the struggle against the Western intelligence services. The fact is that the intelligence war is no ordinary war, here one does not attack with bayonets and combatants do not meet face to face. More often than not the opposing intelligence and counter-intelligence services are far removed from each other and merely carry on the struggle with the help of their secret agents. Therefore, the task before me was not an easy one.

In searching for such an opportunity I pondered over many schemes and rejected them as unsuitable. Some of these schemes are still clear in my memory. At one time, with this aim in view, I had intended to use a citizen of the FRG visiting the GDR. In my official capacity, I had the right to check anyone visiting the GDR from the FRG, using the agent card-index of the KGB and the East German Ministry of Security, in order to tell if he was working for one of those organisations. After making such a check, I could then establish contact with him and prepare the ground for the decisive conversation, the purpose of which was that on return to the FRG he was to inform the BND[1] of my wish to work for them. Theoretically the plan appeared acceptable, from a practical point of view it had drawbacks. First of all, an FRG citizen could have taken such a proposal as a provocation and reported it to the KGB or Ministry of Security. Secondly, people employed in secret services are very cautious and are often afraid of their own shadows. There was no guarantee that the BND would trust me. So I rejected this scheme.

I considered another possibility, a refinement of the first one. I had a very good friend among the East Germans; a reliable, solid person, whom I had known for a long time. He was visited regularly by relatives from the FRG with whom I was also well acquainted. None of them was a KGB agent or an agent of the Ministry of State Security. Through them I could perhaps try to establish contact in the same way, but with American intelligence, who were somewhat more audacious than the BND. However, I rejected this idea also as too many people would be involved and thus make it too risky.

So the first half of 1973 passed, while my undetected attempts to find a plan continued. I still had my duties as a KGB officer to perform, and I had to perform them as well as possible, as this

---

[1] BND—Federal Intelligence of the FRG.

would play an important part in covering my future illegal activity.

At the end of the summer of 1973, KGB officials working in East Germany were informed that following the official recognition of the GDR by a number of countries, it was expected that in the near future embassies and missions representing Western states would be established in East Berlin. It was also stated that the Ministry of Security would assume direct responsibility for work, vis à vis Western embassies in East Berlin.

This information was of great interest to me. Would it be possible to use one of these embassies to establish contact with Western intelligence? Or was there some other way of making contact? In the Soviet Union such action would be suicide. In Moscow, Western embassies are under round-the-clock observation by the KGB. But that was in Moscow. Would the GDR Ministry of Security act in a similar manner in dealing with Western embassies in East Berlin? These were difficult questions to answer. I began to examine the situation, to weigh all the "pros" and "cons".

I learnt that because diplomatic relations had only recently been established with the Western powers, the Ministry of Security was under orders not to harass embassies and staff. This heartened me, but the difficulties were still formidable, since even discreet surveillance of diplomatic premises and personnel could be my undoing. Nevertheless I went on to think out the next steps of my plan.

I knew that even if I succeeded in making contact with embassy officials, it would be no easy task to persuade them that I genuinely wished to help the West fight the evil perversion of "Socialism" imposed by the Communist régimes of Eastern Europe. In the world of intelligence, one must always suspect the trick and the double-bluff. False offers of help are often made in order to try and discover the identities of intelligence officers or their assistants in a diplomatic mission. It is no easy task to persuade people that you have a genuine wish to abandon your "Socialist" masters and help the West. I knew that I must be as open as possible from the beginning, giving full details of my position and role as a KGB officer and that I must ignore the disbelief with which my offer of co-operation was likely to be greeted.

Lastly I turned to the problem of how I could best help once contact had been established. I wished not only to leave behind the profession I had come to hate, but I also wanted to do something to damage the evil system for which I had worked and to atone for some of the misery I had caused. My first thought had been to arrange for my escape and then to take with me all the documents I could when the moment came. However, further thought showed me that the longer I could remain at my post after contact had been made and before defecting, the more I could achieve.

Even when I had decided on the main lines of my plan, the detailed planning and preparation took months to complete. This was not because of my personal position, indeed my power as a KGB officer in East Germany gave me much freedom of movment and action, but because of the intrinsic difficulty in establishing contact, without detection, under the very eyes of my own service and their East German counterparts.

At last all was ready. I knew what I needed to know and I hoped I had planned for all conceivable contingencies. In the life of an intelligence officer, you soon realise that the unlikely and improbable are most likely to happen and you make your plans accordingly.

At this point I should have liked to give a detailed account of how I overcame my difficulties and successfully established contact with a Western intelligence service. However, I cannot, for I know that this book will be read by my masters who will wish to know how I escaped their control. This I must, at all costs, conceal so that others, who may share my experiences of revulsion, will be able to devise their solution and find a way—perhaps the same as mine—to make contact.

Let others be warned that it is not an easy task. But it is not an impossible one, as my presence in the West proves. Risks cannot be elminated, but they can be assessed. If they are too great, then the scheme must be abandoned and another one found. The way I chose worked, and I hope that my silence about it will keep that way safe for others.

Now I will return to the early days of 1974, shortly before the point at which I started this account. I had already been in contact with the West for a period of time, when I began to sense that all was not well. Usually matters of intelligence work can be dealt with by carefully following your training and the methods of work you have been taught. But sometimes one must act on instinct. I tried to suppress my forebodings but the feeling got worse. I felt sure I had only a short time left. Accordingly I began to make final preparations for my escape to the West. My Western contacts wished to help me but I understood that the situation placed the main burden of preparation on my shoulders.

To this end I intended utilising an excursion by officers of the 16th Motorised Rifle Regiment to West Berlin. They made excursions like this regularly several times a year in order to study American, British and French military installations there. They had to be accompanied by a KGB officer and on their next visit it would be my turn. The dates of the excursions to West Berlin were fixed by an officer on the staff of the 6th Guards Division who was a good acquaintance of mine. I asked him if he was planning a visit to West Berlin in the near future for a group of officers. Of course, he could not give a negative reply to a request from a KGB official, especially one with whom he was acquainted. A trip was planned by him for the beginning of the next month, in fact for 2 February 1974.

About a week before the trip I had a prearranged meeting with my Western contact. Because of the great danger associated with face-to-face meeting, these were kept to a minimum and communication was usually by other means. This one was absolutely vital. But I still had that feeling of foreboding. About ten minutes after we parted, my worst expectations were justified. I was being followed. The feeling that they are hunting you down like a wild animal is extremely unpleasant. My heart beat faster; the palms of my hand became clammy. Not from fear; I felt no fear, but it was anticipation of the struggle ahead. For me it was a question of life and death and in such a situation fear is a bad companion. He who is afraid cannot think clearly and loses.

"Don't worry, don't worry," I repeated to myself. "In a situation like this, only sensible decisions can save you." Then I thought: "What do my pursuers want from me? Of course they will want to establish my address; that is what they will need." After establishing my address, the Ministry of State Security would then arrange to place me under total surveillance, discover who I was and then hand over the material to the KGB. This would mean arrest, prison and perhaps even the firing squad. It was not a cheerful prospect.

Whatever happened I had to evade surveillance. But I had to be patient. If my pursuers noticed that I had discovered them and was trying to give them the slip, then they would possibly simply arrest me and, as a Soviet citizen, hand me straight over to the KGB. That would be the same again in the end, prison or shooting. Therefore I must remain calm and pretend that I had not noticed that I was under surveillance at all. By behaving in such a way I wanted to show my pursuers how inexperienced I was in matters of intelligence and counter-intelligence, thereby increasing their hopes of an easy success and causing them to relax their attention. Then, using the onset of darkness, exploiting the element of surprise and resorting to various ruses, I planned to evade surveillance.

There were still three hours remaining before it became dark and I started to wander around the centre of Berlin with a carefree air, pausing at shop windows and at various kiosks. It suddenly occurred to me that I could introduce myself to a girl, my roam around Berlin would then not appear aimless to a bystander but completely normal and explicable and to some extent would confuse my pursuers. I liked this idea and after about 15 minutes was chatting away animatedly to a cheerful young Berlin girl and paying her innumerable compliments which she, of course, hardly believed but which, fortunately for me, she listened to willingly.

So time slipped by and it began to get dark. I could no longer see my pursuers; evidently they were satisfied that they had me covered and had withdrawn some distance away from me. I was glad and quickly said goodbye to the young woman, ignoring her obvious disappointment.

"But I thought we could go somewhere and dance," she said, stretching out her hand.

"Next time without fail," I replied and thought that "dance" was exactly what I was going to have to do.

I walked around the corner and then began to run as fast as I possibly could. I was counting on surprise and speed. I vaulted several fences and ran down several dark passage ways, careered around the streets and parks like a madman. After about 30 to 40 minutes of this I could see nothing of my pursuers. They could not keep up with the mad race. I had left them behind somewhere in the darkness.

"You should keep fit," I said aloud and maliciously about my lagging pursuers. I slowed down to a brisk walk and headed for an S-Bahn station where I caught a train back towards the centre of Berlin. Three stations before my destination I got out of the train and completed the journey, about eight kilometres, on foot across fields and woods in order to make finally and absolutely sure that there was no one following me.

I knew I was now nearly at the end of the line. What would be there for me would depend on my own efforts and much good luck. The longest days of my life passed at last, the 2nd of February came, and the same night I was flying out of Berlin on a British aircraft, with an escort of fighters, on my way to freedom. I had taken on the KGB, and won!

SECRET

APPENDIX I

1 February 1968

COUNTER-INTELLIGENCE WORK OF THE STATE SECURITY ORGANS OF THE USSR

1. Subject of course
2. Dialectical materialism as the methodological basis of the course.
3. System of the course.
4. Place of course SD-1 in the system of other SDs.

1. A worldwide Socialist system is the decisive factor for the political and economic development of the world. The balance of power has shifted in favour of Socialism, but nothing can happen by itself and victory can only be achieved through struggle. Aggressive forces are raising a tremendous resistance to the growth of Socialist power—growth-resistance.

Imperialists assign a foremost place to their intelligence services, which are global and total in character, and they continue to improve them. *The main weapon of these services is the agent network.*

In these circumstances, the Soviet Government is compelled to employ State Security organs. According to the 1968 statutes *State Security organs are political organs* responsible for defence against internal and foreign enemies, and their basic purpose does not merely involve technical means of defence or the use of arms, but in methods of resolving political problems. The policy of State Security organs is drawn up by the Communist Party according to the existing situation.

Its activities are threefold:

1. Administrative.
2. Operational: intelligence and counter-intelligence.
3. Investigative.

Operational activities of State Security organs: This is intelligence activity in the widest sense of the word. Intelligence activity becomes operational when directed towards the fight against intruders, its purpose being to obtain information on the adversary and to sabotage his endeavours. Intelligence presupposes a cunning and clandestine method of action, which is achieved through camouflage. The main weapon is the agent network.

Counter-intelligence complements the work of intelligence. In this connection the work divides in two spheres: work within the country, collation of data, and so on; while simultaneously, the counter-intelligence staff will establish their own network in the intelligence services of the enemy. This will provide information.

SECRET

SECRET

It must be borne in mind that Socialist countries' intelligence services are basically different. *Intelligence services of Socialist states emerged from the victory of revolutionary violence and are directed to the defence of workers' interests.* Blackmail, etc., is not used. Soviet intelligence and counter-intelligence officers work whole-heartedly. Soviet intelligence is fighting against enemies.

Intelligence activity is divided into several fields:

1. *Political intelligence.*
2. *Economic intelligence.*
3. *Scientific-technical intelligence.*

Science makes the transition from superstructure to basics. Military intelligence. Counter-intelligence on a wide scale. Operational work is not limited to tasks only, *but includes educational work* aimed at people who could fall into criminal ways. State Security organs conduct many-sided organisational activities with the masses.

Subject of the course: objective conformity to law in the struggle waged by State Security organs against subversive activities of imperialist intelligence services, and of anti-Soviet elements within the country.

2. *Dialectical materialism as the methodological basis of the course.* Dialectical materialism, being the overall method of scientific knowledge, also serves as the method for counter-intelligence courses. It reveals the fact that operational activities are profoundly conditioned by the foreign and internal policies of the Soviet State and depend on the international situation and its correct evaluation. In many cases, one must rely only on one's own knowledge. In the process of study, dialectics will help to co-ordinate the theory and practice of operational work and to analyse and present a scientific picture of the work. A counter-intelligence course must be based on scientific tenets and deductions, on knowledge of the laws of class struggle.

Great attention is to be paid to political training. Lagging makes for apathy; work uninterruptedly in support of the dictatorship of the proletariat. Counter-intelligence work is directed against real, active adversaries, including some who may be unknown to us. Political convictions are of decisive strength also when working within the country.

3. *Content of the system of the course.* This consists of knowledge, work and acquired practices: intelligence service against intelligence service with the latest intelligence activities. Knowledge consists of factual data, theoretical contentions, principles and rules of counter-intelligence activity.

SECRET

SECRET

APPENDIX II

2 February 1968

MAIN TASKS AND DIRECTION OF COUNTER-INTELLIGENCE WORK OF STATE SECURITY ORGANS AT THE PRESENT STAGE

1. Tasks of counter-intelligence networks.
2. Main directions of counter-intelligence work.

The forces of Soviet society are headed and directed by the CPSU. The Party illuminates the Soviet people's path in the struggle for the victory of Communism; it guides and directs all their forces. The organs of State Security are also directed by the CPSU.

The 22nd and 23rd Party Congresses emphasised the necessity to strengthen State Security; to maintain vigilance, and the importance of increasing political activity. In the future also, the CPSU is going to increase the vigilance of the Soviet people. At the present stage, the guiding role of the Party is growing in every sphere, including the work of State Security.

At the 1966 October Plenum, a special question was raised in regard to stepping up the work of State Security in connection with the international situation (events in Greece and the Middle East). The basic aims and tasks for ensuring State Security result from the resolutions of the Congresses: active opposition to imperialist intelligence services and protection of USSR's state frontiers.

In the present circumstances, State Security tasks are determined by foreign and internal factors. As today's international situation is complex and dynamic, methods of State Security work must remain flexible. On the one hand, Socialist forces are growing and getting stronger, but on the other the imperialist forces of the USA and the Federal German Republic are stepping up their aggressive policy. They spare no means, and this pressure, therefore, must be repulsed.

A determining factor is the foreign policy of the Soviet Government. Another factor is the increasing role of the imperialist intelligence services. In their subversive activities, the imperialist powers come up against the fact that internal forces are working to make the aims of imperialist intelligence more and more impossible, and they are, therefore, obliged to engage in the formation of sabotage units. In the period of Socialism, the Socialist system has been realised, but it must be borne in mind that intelligence services can make use of certain shortcomings, survivals of the past, anti-Soviet attitudes, carelessness, talkativeness, and imitativeness; these factors have some bearing on State Security work. The determining factors are the

SECRET

SECRET

international and internal situations.

The 1967 June Plenum gave instructions to increase vigilance, to devote more attention to the work of the security organs. Thus State Security workers even in peacetime must work in a special way, remaining on the alert at all times. Tasks must be set for a sharp increase in political intelligence obtained from the enemy's camp. Active counter-intelligence offensives must be launched; the despatching of agents is not to be delayed. Facilities of the different State Security organs must be fully utilised.

The 1966 December Plenum stressed that intelligence and counter-intelligence must not limit themselves to separate spheres of action.

KGB Directive No. 43 of 1967 to the counter-intelligence services gave instructions to take active measures for discovering and foiling enemy schemes, and so on. It is essential to take account of increasing imperialist activity on the ideological front, which is not simply slander but a refined and expert course of action.

1. Tasks of counter-intelligence networks are determinded by Committee regulations. The organs are trained as skilled political organs. Counter-intelligence networks are faced with a series of tasks:
    1. Fighting against spying, sabotage, terrorism and other activities of the imperialist intelligence services. The prime effort must be directed against the main enemies: the USA, West Germany, England, France.
    2. Safeguarding the Soviet Army, Navy, Border Forces and MVD Forces from penetration by capitalist intelligence networks and hostile elements.

MILITARY COUNTER-INTELLIGENCE REGULATIONS, SEPTEMBER 1961 No. 00270 OF 8 SEPTEMBER 1961 ISSUED BY THE CHAIRMAN: 'RIGHTS AND DUTIES GOVERNING RELATIONS WITH LOCAL UNITS AND COMMANDERS'

Duties of Special Departments [00]
1. To prevent enemy agent networks from penetrating into units and establishments of the Soviet Army, Navy, KGB and MOOP Forces.
2. To identify and unmask agents and others who have penetrated the armed forces.
3. To search for imperialist agents amongst the armed forces and their immediate surroundings. (Indications observed, facts, relatives.)

SECRET

SECRET

4. To avert cases of treason to the motherland by individual servicemen, workers, and employees of units and establishments.

5. To ensure the preservation of state and military secrets and to sever channels of leakage of secret information abroad.

6. To prepare and carry out, together with State Security [OGB] and Ministry of Defence [MO] organs, special measures for disinformation of the enemy, for recording, and for camouflaging especially important military objectives.

7. Fullest co-operation to be given to commanders and political organs for increasing vigilance.

8. To carry out special missions for the Central Committee of the CPSU and the Soviet Government.

9. Counter-intelligence work on special and particularly important targets and on transport.

10. Suppression of hostile actions of anti-Soviet and nationalist elements within the country.

11. Protection of the state borders of the USSR.

12. Protection of the leadership of the CPSU and the Soviet Government.

All State Security counter-intelligence work is carried out according to policy directions from above.

2. Main directions of State Security counter-intelligence work. At the foundation of strategy and tactics stands the requirement . . . to direct KGB and State Security activities to the outside, against the intelligence services of the imperialist powers.

1. Fight against the subversive activity of intelligence centres, residenturas, anti-Soviet centres abroad, intelligence officers and agents. Fight against ideological sabotage (ways to identify and suppress), also against spying and subversive actions of those serving under official cover of an embassy or . . . of a representation. Identification of persons suspected of belonging to the above category by means of a secure watch kept on state borders, search for hostile agents and . . . illegals. Identify intelligence officers arriving among other foreigners in order to recruit; collect information and establish communications. Our men travel abroad in order to safeguard the security of our people. By planting an agent network in an intelligence service, we intercept the communications channels (operational games[1] with adversary). 5th Department. The fight against

---

[1] Or plays.

SECRET

SECRET

ideological sabotage is sharpened by the inflammatory activities of China.

2. Obtaining of intelligence information in the course of operational work of counter-intelligence networks.

3. Fight against subversive activity of anti-Soviet elements within the country. *A complex of questions.* Identify and unmask anti-Soviet manifestations of Ukrainian, Lithuanian, Estonian, Latvian nationalists. Break off capitalist gains from the influence of VATCHMAN[2], which is a very flexible organisation. Search for instigators of anti-Soviet elements.

4. Fight against criminal intrusions on the security of particularly important targets in military industries and other installations of special importance. Ensure the safety of state and military secrets.

5. Prepare conditions for active State Security counter-intelligence work at special times and for the repelling of possible aggression of imperialist powers against the USSR.

Sources: *Textbook of Organisation of Counter-intelligence Work.* Summary of lecture. KBG Collection of writings 1967, No 2. Articles by heads of Special Departments and Epishev's article 'Basis of Counter-intelligence Activity of KGB Organs'.

---

[2] The meaning of this phrase is somewhat doubtful.

SECRET

APPENDIX III

REPORT

ON WAYS, METHODS AND DEVICES USED BY AGENTS OF WESTERN INTELLIGENCE SERVICES FOR THE COLLECTION OF INTELLIGENCE INFORMATION ON THE GSFG [GROUP OF SOVIET FORCES IN GERMANY] 2/D — 38 SS
THE ASPIRATIONS OF IMPERIALIST INTELLIGENCE SERVICES AS REGARDS THE GSFG

Special attention is given to obtaining information on the most important changes taking place in the armed forces, on signs of tension, as well as the absence of any such signs. The enemy attaches the greatest importance to information on the following:

1. Missile units.
2. Air Force and anti-aircraft units and formations.
3. Large railway junctions, railway stations used for loading and unloading of troops and equipment.
4. Branch lines running alongside military zones.
5. All kinds of tanks, artillery installations, special means of transport: tractors, including those without missiles; all special vehicles; generators, charging and compressor installations, radar stations, infra-red devices, and other things.
6. All newly built military complexes.
7. Firing ranges, bombing areas, river-crossing points.
8. All kinds of workshops for the repair of weapons and equipment.
9. Depots and stores for weapons, ammunition and food.
10. Main roads constantly being used by troops and which go to firing ranges and concentration areas.
11. Radio-relay networks and lines of the GSFG which are covered by the apparatus of an anti-aircraft system.
12. Lines of air-liaison going to military installations, location of cables, thickness and number of wires in a cable.

The recruiting attempts of enemy Intelligence Services vis-à-vis Soviet citizens which are aimed at military personnel:

1. Staff Officers.
2. Missile and radar personnel, and pilots.
3. Officers responsible for bringing the armed forces to a heightened state of battle readiness and those responsible for the supplying of units with ammunition.

SECRET

SECRET

4. Military doctors.
5. Soviet citizens who have contacts with local inhabitants.
Special attention is devoted to persons who are:
6. Dissatisfied with their jobs.
7. In the habit of over-indulging in alcoholic drinks.
8. In contact with German women.
9. Greedy for money.
10. Admirers of the Western way of life, greedy for material possessions. (All this being done with a view to intensifying these vices even further.)

The enemy also considers the following *factors to be conducive to recruitment:*

1. Critical attitude towards Soviet reality.
2. Excessive ambition.
3. Breakdown in family life or marriage.
4. Tendency to indulge in alcoholic drinks.

Individual Soviet Military personnel can come to the attention of the Western Special Intelligence Services:

1. As a result of contacts with foreigners in the territory of the USSR, before being posted to the GSFG, or while at home on leave.
2. From material based on questions put by repatriates, as well as private businessmen visiting the USSR or the GDR.
3. By publishing scientific or other articles in the open press.
4. As a result of leads followed up by Intelligence organs.
5. By sending letters of a slanderous or anti-Soviet character to *Svoboda* [Freedom newspaper] and other publications.
6. Under influence of relatives or other contacts living in capitalist countries.
7. On the basis of *intimate relations with women* who are agents of foreign Intelligence Services.
8. As a result of marrying German women with relatives living in the West.
9. As a result of amoral behaviour, speculative deals, conspicuous peculiar behaviour, work missing operations and so on.
10. As a result of frequenting civilian [word missing] in East Berlin.

Places which may be used by enemy Intelligence Services for studying Soviet citizens for the purpose of eventual recruitment:

1. In establishments where official meetings take place between representatives of enemy Armed Forces and Soviet Military personnel.

SECRET

SECRET

2. In places where Soviet citizens meet with German commercial firms and/or other German organisations to arrange food and other supply questions.
3. During unofficial contacts and visits to taverns, restaurants, shops, cinemas.
4. Directly within Soviet military installations which have been penetrated by Western intelligence agencies, through Germans who are working there.
5. In Officers Club.
6. In buildings where Soviet Liaison Missions are located.
7. In places where international gatherings take place (Leipzig, Erfurt).
8. In Sanatoria (Bad Emster).

Attempts to recruit agents from amongst the local population are aimed at those:

1. Working in Soviet military institutions.
2. Residing in the vicinity of Soviet military installations.
3. Working in building-firms, motor-car repairs or other repair services.
4. Working at railway stations.
5. Connected with servicing Soviet citizens, e.g. tailor-shops.
6. Women of easy virtue or prostitutes.

Some revealing traits in the behaviour of enemy agents:

1. Regular visits to areas in the vicinity of Soviet military installations.
2. Regular journeys outside the confines of his usual place of residence.
3. Ascertaining that the suspected person dispatches mail posted in a place outside his place of residence.
4. Posting to West Germany of printed matter—newspapers not having a political bent.
5. Receiving letters from West Germany.
6. Finding on the suspected person town-maps printed by the firm Dewag (with a grid).
7. Establishing friendly relations with persons residing at military installations.
8. Journeys to Socialist countries (Yugoslavia, Cuba).
9. Posting letters to the following addresses in West Germany: BND, Baden-Wurtenberg, Halderberg, Mannheim; American and French Intelligence in West Berlin; Department for the Defence of the Constitution in West Berlin, Cologne, Aachen, Hamburg, Bonn, Wuppertal, Ragen.

SECRET

SECRET

Characteristic behavioural patterns in an agent engaged in visual observation:

1. General nervousness, constrained movements, frequent looking over one's shoulder.
2. Aim to leave quickly the place being observed.
3. Haste in showing documents justifying presence at a Soviet military installation.
4. Confused replies regarding the reason for presence at a Soviet military installation.

Some revealing traits in the actions of an agent receiving one-way transmissions or engaged in radio communications:

1. Keeping awake two nights running (at times of crisis, etc.).
2. Ascertaining the fact of postal correspondence being dispatched immediately after the day fixed for radio transmission.
3. Discovery of his definite frequencies, note-books with five-figure groups.
4. Presence in the attic, in his room or in a shed of large aerials erected for transmission, or of insulated pieces of wire which could be used as an aerial.
5. Use of headphones.
6. Creating the impression that the suspected person is absent from the flat at the time of reception.
7. Refusal to receive visitors especially on the days of reception.
8. Recording radio broadcasts on a tape-recorder.
9. Concealment of knowledge in radio matters.

Some instructions given by enemy Intelligence to their agents engaged in visual observation:

1. Not to allow any change to take place in either public or private way of life when beginning intelligence activities.
2. Conceal sympathy for Western way of life.
3. React calmly to all provocations from various people.
4. Not to establish contacts with obvious enemies of East Germany.
5. Before visiting the target to be observed, prepare cover story.
6. Go to the target to be observed accompanied by family.
7. Not to carry out observation always wearing the same clothes and to go there at various times of day.
8. Not to allow any notes to be made while in the area of the military installation.
9. Not to carry out observation during week-ends.
10. Visit the target on days of holiday (Red Army Day, May-Day, November).

SECRET

SECRET

11. For more prolonged observation of the target, make use of a non-working activity (sun-bathing, all sorts of walks).
12. Targets to which access is difficult are to be observed in the guise of mushroom-pickers, etc.
13. Make observations of firing ranges and training.
14. Visit Soviet troops and stores.
15. Make use of suitably-located windows of your flat.
16. Exposure of agents and illegals amongst specialist-military personnel serving with NATO operating in areas surrounding military installations.

Established means of agent dispatch:

1. Under cover of returnees.
2. Going over to East Germany in the guise of deserters from the Bundeswehr [Armed Forces, FRG].
3. In the guise of sailors on West German ships, leaving the ship on arrival in an East German port.
4. Illegal crossing of the border.

Instructions given to "Rangers":

1. Not to do anything which would attract attention or give cause for investigating past background (not to enlist in the East German State Security Service, not to aim at rewards).
2. Behave in a loyal manner towards the GDR.

Give-away signs identifying an agent of enemy Intelligence, planted by the latter on our own Intelligence Agencies:

1. Too hasty investigation of West German authorities into agent's anti-Government attitudes.
2. Mention of relatives or friends working in various secret establishments.
3. Suggestions for a meeting by the agent which follow all rules of conspiracy or otherwise.
4. Target himself invites recruitment.
5. In writing down a message, target leaves a clear field at the top, without having first received instructions to do so, etc.
6. On being given a definite task, target finds it difficult to give an answer.
7. Target himself offering to do various things on own initiative.

SECRET